MY ONE-OF-A-KIND BODY

The Ultimate Guide to Caring for Me

Whitney Casares, MD, MPH, FAAP

American Academy of Pediatrics
DEDICATED TO THE HEALTH OF ALL CHILDREN®

American Academy of Pediatrics Publishing Staff

Mark Grimes, *Vice President, Publishing*
Jeff Mahony, *Senior Director, Professional and Consumer Publishing*
Holly Kaminski, *Editor, Consumer Publishing*
Grace Klooster, *Editorial Assistant*
Jason Crase, *Senior Manager, Production and Editorial Services*
Shannan Martin, *Production Manager, Consumer Publications*
Soraya Alem, *Manager, Digital Publishing*
Sara Hoerdeman, *Marketing and Acquisitions Manager, Consumer Products*

Published by the American Academy of Pediatrics
345 Park Blvd
Itasca, IL 60143
Telephone: 630/626-6000
Facsimile: 847/434-8000
www.aap.org

The American Academy of Pediatrics is an organization of 67,000 primary care pediatricians, pediatric medical subspecialists, and pediatric surgical specialists dedicated to the health, safety, and well-being of all infants, children, adolescents, and young adults.

The information contained in this publication should not be used as a substitute for the medical care and advice of your pediatrician. There may be variations in treatment that your pediatrician may recommend based on individual facts and circumstances.

Statements and opinions expressed are those of the author and not necessarily those of the American Academy of Pediatrics.

Any websites, brand names, products, or manufacturers are mentioned for informational and identification purposes only and do not imply an endorsement by the American Academy of Pediatrics (AAP). The AAP is not responsible for the content of external resources. Information was current at the time of publication.

The publishers have made every effort to trace the copyright holders for borrowed materials. If they have inadvertently overlooked any, they will be pleased to make the necessary arrangements at the first opportunity.

This publication has been developed by the American Academy of Pediatrics. The contributors are expert authorities in the field of pediatrics. No commercial involvement of any kind has been solicited or accepted in the development of the content of this publication. Disclosures: Dr. Casares has disclosed financial relationships as a consultant with Gerber and as a consultant with CeraVe. Any other disclosures were reviewed and determined not relevant to the work related to *My One-of-a-Kind Body*—consumer book aimed at preteens focusing on body positivity and acceptance. Disclosures are reviewed and mitigated through a Conflict-of-Interest process that consists of reviewing pertinent information which is then used to decide what action is required to maintain content integrity. There may be instances where no action is necessary. This process has been approved by the AAP Board of Directors.

Every effort is made to keep *My One-of-a-Kind Body: The Ultimate Guide to Caring for Me* consistent with the most recent advice and information available from the American Academy of Pediatrics.

Special discounts are available for bulk purchases of this publication. Email Special Sales at nationalaccounts@aap.org for more information.

Printed in the United States of America
9-523/0925   2 3 4 5 6 7 8 9 10
CB0142
ISBN: 978-1-61002-803-5
eBook: 978-1-61002-804-2
EPUB: 978-1-61002-805-9

Cover design and illustrations by Lisa Perrett
Publication design by Scott Rattray Design

Library of Congress Control Number: 2024949197

Also Available for Kids From the American Academy of Pediatrics

You-ology: A Puberty Guide for EVERY Body

Additional Books for Parents of Preteens and Teens From the American Academy of Pediatrics

ADHD: What Every Parent Needs to Know

Autism Spectrum Disorder: What Every Parent Needs to Know

Building Happier Kids: Stress-busting Tools for Parents

Building Resilience in Children and Teens: Giving Kids Roots and Wings

Caring for Your School-Age Child: Ages 5-12

Congrats—You're Having a Teen! Strengthen Your Family and Raise a Good Person

Digging Into Nature: Outdoor Adventures for Happier and Healthier Kids

Family Fit Plan: A 30-Day Wellness Transformation

High Five Discipline: Positive Parenting for Happy, Healthy, Well-Behaved Kids

Lighthouse Parenting: Raising Your Child With Loving Guidance for a Lifelong Bond

Nurturing Boys to Be Better Men: Gender Equality Starts at Home

Parenting Through Puberty: Mood Swings, Acne, and Growing Pains

Quirky Kids: Understanding and Supporting Your Child With Developmental Differences

Raising an Organized Child: 5 Steps to Boost Independence, Ease Frustration, and Promote Confidence

To find additional AAP books for parents, visit **aap.org/shopaap-for-parents, amazon.com/americanacademyofpediatrics,** or your favorite bookseller or library.

aap.org/shopaap

For more pediatrician-approved advice and the latest updates, visit **HealthyChildren.org, the official AAP website for parents.**

For my daughters—and for every child learning to trust their body, care for it with compassion, and celebrate the superpower of being one of a kind.

CONTENTS

A MESSAGE FOR PARENTS

As parents, our primary job is to keep our children safe and healthy. When they're little, we teach them how to tie their shoes, ride a bike, and cross the street. As they grow older, we're responsible for making sure they learn how to manage money, avoid illness, and function successfully at school. Every day we teach them how to build their social, academic, and emotional regulation skills like deep breathing, naming our emotions, and taking space when we need it. We're constantly investing in their future selves. Teaching our children to love their bodies is just as important as all the other ways we promote their health throughout their lives. It can be tricky, though, to know exactly how to do that in the world we live in today. Even as a **pediatrician** dedicated to instilling positive body image in my own young daughters, navigating the constant messages they receive about their physical appearances, teaching them to give their bodies all the fuel and movement they need, and fully unwinding my own internal body image programming can sometimes be a challenge. And if it's a challenge for me as a maternal child health expert, I know it's a challenge for every other parent too.

Our kids are exposed to toxic body image messages at younger and younger ages. They see photoshopped images in ads on television and in print; they're pressured to buy expensive, age-inappropriate skin care products by peers; and (given it's impossible for most parents to completely block access) they can be exposed to harmful content on social media. There's no way for their generation to fully escape social media's influence or even the beauty standards of their peers. Body consciousness is everywhere. Children as young as 3 years expressed body confidence issues in a recent study, and according to the National Institutes of Health, almost half of kids and teens have body image issues. Conflicting messages about body love and body ideals fill our smartphones; everywhere we look, photoshopped images of painfully thin, airbrushed women who seemingly have no pores and male models with perfectly sculpted muscles, coiffed in-place locks, and paper-white teeth sit juxtaposed next to thought pieces extolling us to love our bodies even if they don't look like those unrealistic standards. Commentary about aging gracefully sits front and center in the media, alongside pictures of youth regeneration serums.

What's more, most parents' relationships with their own bodies are fraught. We're still scarred from the grapefruit diets, workout videos, SlimFast trends, and low-fat crazes of our youth. We still recall *America's Next Top Model* episodes, remembering how the judges criticized each contestant, picking apart their hair, skin, and facial structures. The images of hulky sports heroes or acne-free celebrities we longed to emulate in our preteen years live rent free in our adult minds. We still hear our own mothers (or fathers) body shaming themselves in the mirror as we, young, impressionable children, watched on. And even if we don't want to pass on toxic diet culture thoughts and habits to our own kids, that's a lot easier said than done. In a recent study published in the *International Journal of Eating Disorders,* researchers found that 76% of parents with preadolescents or adolescents had denigrated their own bodies in front of their children, and 43.6% commented on their kids' bodies. Pile on seemingly at-odds advice about body positivity versus the importance of maintaining a healthy body mass index (BMI), and it all becomes muddy real fast. That's why in this book, we'll focus on making the landscape of body confidence a whole lot clearer for kids, showing how to feel positive about whatever body they're in while, at the same time, teaching them to take care of the only body they've got.

Your child will meet some characters in *My One-of-a-Kind Body* that will remind them of themselves and a bunch who will challenge them to understand others' life experiences. We'll help kids realize that building consistent healthy habits around physical and mental health is the most successful way to love their bodies and that they can navigate whatever messages they see and hear about their bodies, whatever body that is—if they remember a few key principles.

- We can be proud of our unique, sometimes awkward, and totally amazing bodies. As humans, our differences are what make us special—and that includes how we look. As bodies grow, they change, and then they change again. It's supposed to be that way.
- Most current body ideals are rooted in racism, sexism, and old standards. "Fat," "blemish free," "kinky hair," "short," and "tall" are all just words. We only think of some words as good and some as bad because that's what we've been told for such a long time. In reality, if a person is significantly underweight or has disordered eating that leads to anorexia or bulimia, they can face severe health risks, just like someone can if they live in a larger body. If kids have blemish-free skin because they scrub too hard or use products that disrupt the skin barrier, their skin isn't healthy, it's damaged. If someone subscribes to the idea that they *need* to undergo plastic surgery procedures to "fix" their natural appearance (and to be worthy of love and acceptance), it can come with a costly emotional price tag.
- BMI (a calculation used in the medical field to define diagnoses like underweight, overweight, and obesity) is a commonly used vital sign for health, but it's also a flawed tool, rooted in racism and inferior to other measures of health.
- Our body doesn't need to be fixed because it's not broken. It does need to be taken care of, though, because it's the only one we'll ever have.

Although the messages within are aimed primarily at supporting our kids, parents will also learn their role in promoting their children's health. You'll be reminded about the ways over-commenting on your body, and on your child's body, affects your kids deeply. You'll see how experts recommend celebrating and caring for *all* bodies—kids who are neurodivergent, kids who have a disability, kids who are medically complex, kids of all different races and backgrounds, kids with all different body sizes, and kids with all kinds of family structures. You'll hear firsthand how constructive body-related talk sounds, and we'll teach you how to model body confidence. Finally, we'll walk through how to work with your child's pediatrician as a true team member when it comes to communicating health information to you and your child, as well as keeping your child safe and healthy—my ultimate job as a pediatrician, and our ultimate job as parents.

As a pediatrician I share common questions kids ask me when they feel awkward about their bodies. It's important for kids to feel confident in asking you or their pediatrician questions that weigh on their mind. The responses I provide are excellent examples for you to use when you're unsure of how to respond to your child's worries, questions, and body statements too. Feel free to steal those responses and make them your own!

CHAPTER 1

MEET THE CHARACTERS

You are going to love this book! I am telling you I wrote this book just for you, you, and you! I wrote it for my own kids, their friends, and all my patients who come to visit me when they are sick or have questions. I wrote this book for my nieces, nephews, and the kids in my neighborhood. I have even written this for all the kids I have never met before. Even though we have never met before, I know we have one thing in common. Can you guess what it is? If you shouted out "BODY!" you are correct. I have one, you have one, and so do all the other kids reading this book. What makes this fun is that none of our bodies are the same. You might be tall and skinny, you might be short with freckles, you might wear glasses and have really long hair or even a mohawk. You might have pale skin or dark hair, you might wear a hijab or a yarmulke, you might spend your days in a wheelchair or be the fastest sprinter on your block. Whatever type of body you have, however you look, whoever you are—you have a body that needs and deserves respect and care.

As your body grows things happen. Your pits might get stinky. Your breath might smell if you forget to brush your teeth. Your body will burp and fart at all the wrong times! Your stomach will rumble during class when you're hungry. Snot rockets might fly out of your nose by accident when you sneeze. You'll most definitely have a bad hair day when your locks decide they're in charge, not your hairbrush. You'll get food stuck in your braces, earwax on your fingers, and nose hairs that poke out right on school picture day. No worries! I'm here to walk you through how to feel good in your own skin even when it feels like you're the only one whose body isn't as perfect as it should be (because—*spoiler alert*—everyone feels that way sometimes) and even when it feels like your body is changing into something you don't recognize anymore (because—*spoiler alert*—that's what's supposed to happen as you grow up).

While our bodies may look different from each other, we all grow up with one. So, it's very important to learn how to take care of it and appreciate all it does for us every day! In this book, you'll meet 5 kids who are all incredibly different from each other—Greta, Juan, Natalia, Hayley, and Troy. They have different family structures, different body shapes and sizes, different cultures, and different day-to-day lives, but they're all learning important lessons about caring for their bodies, just like you are. As you read this book you will notice some words in **blue**. These blue words might be tricky, so more information on these words will be provided in the Glossary in the back of the book.

Juan

is a 12-year-old boy who lives in Texas with his mom and dad. He loves and plays all kinds of sports, but football is his favorite. Juan hasn't ever left his home state, but he wants to travel all across the country one day visiting all the stadiums where his favorite teams play. His dream is to be a professional football player—and maybe a sportscaster one day too!

Natalia

is an 11-year-old kid with cerebral palsy who lives in New York City. Their favorite food is pizza. They've used a wheelchair since they were 3 years old. Sometimes, when they don't want to use their wheelchair, they use their arm braces. Natalia is a New York pizza expert. They can tell you where all the best crispy crust spots are in their neighborhood and in the rest of New York's boroughs as well.

Hayley

is a 9-year-old gymnast who spends half her time with her dad and half her time with her mom. She spends most of the week practicing gymnastics and loves to read outside when the weather's nice in Michigan. She's not sure if she really likes gymnastics, but her mom was a gymnast when she was young, so it's kind of a family tradition. Sometimes she wishes she had more free time, but it feels like right when one gymnastics season is done, it's time to start getting ready for a new one!

Troy

is a 10-year-old boy who plays clarinet in the school band where he lives with his dad in California. He wants to be a Southern chef when he grows up using all the recipes his grandma taught him in her kitchen. His cat, Fitzgerald, is his best friend. Troy loves jazz music most, but he's also into funk, soul, and rhythm and blues.

CHAPTER 2

CAMPFIRES AND CORAZONES

Pop, pop, pop. Tiny flames of light crackled up high, high, higher into the smoky campfire air, the stars a little hazy. They looked like they were blinking off and on in the night sky as Greta, Juan, Natalia, Hayley, and Troy watched them flicker. These summer camp nights seemed to go on forever—or at least all 5 kids wished they would. It had been one of the best weeks of their lives, full of lake swimming, field games, cabin time, and nights like this, sitting around a campfire singing silly songs and roasting marshmallows. Camp Corazón means "Camp Heart" in Spanish, and the kids had fallen in love with everything about this sleepaway camp, perched high in the mountains of Pennsylvania.

Tomorrow they'd all go back to their homes across the country, but for now they snuggled up around the fire, grateful for their new friendships and happy to have pen pals to write to about anything they wanted to once real life started back again in the fall (even if "writing" meant sending a text message here or there on their parents' phones). Greta and Natalia had bonded over the specialists they saw once a month to keep their medical needs on track. Juan and Hayley connected quickly once they realized how big a role sports played in their lives. Troy had them all dancing in the mess hall and after each meal on their way back to their cabins. They were all so different, but they had all learned so much from each other.

"Promise to write me?" Natalia asked Greta, holding up the friendship bracelet on their wrist. It read "T-R-U-E♥F-R-I-E-N-D-S" in brightly colored beads.

"Totally!" Greta exclaimed, pulling back the sleeve of her camp sweatshirt to reveal her matching one. "My dads said they would let me use their phone to contact you when they're home and we want to catch up. BFFs for life?"

"For always!" they exclaimed. "Forever!"

Juan, Hayley, and Troy echoed their new buddies' excitement.

"Forever and for always!"

✷ ✷ ✷ ✷ ✷

One month later, Natalia was sitting in their apartment, feeling like they were a million miles away from that happy campfire moment. They were confused about something a classmate, Neil, said about their body that morning at school. Natalia has **cerebral palsy,** a condition that affects movement, muscle coordination, and posture. Some kids, like Natalia, use a wheelchair. Natalia had been using a wheelchair since before they could remember, so they were used to people sometimes looking awkwardly at them or asking questions about their life. It was part of the deal. But today, Neil said something more personal—and it made Natalia feel uncomfortable.

The 2 friends were in the hallway talking about their favorite foods when Neil said that he loved the veggie samosas and curries that his grandma made. "We Patels know how to eat! Do you eat *anything,* Natalia? You need to put some meat on those bones! You're way too skinny—like a little beanpole."

Yael, Natalia's closest friend at school, just happened to be coming around the corner when she heard Neil's comments. Yael knew what it was like to be teased about the foods you ate. In her family, there was no pork allowed. Sometimes at pizza parties, kids would make a big deal about her not eating pepperoni and ham. She'd explained her family's religious food restrictions a million times.

"Neil, that's not kind at all," Yael said, throwing her arm around Natalia's shoulders. "We're all different and what we eat is too."

What Neil didn't know was that because Natalia's cerebral palsy influenced their ability to chew, swallow, and digest food, they'd always been thin. Their doctor had been working with them to make sure they grew well for their whole life. It was so much work—work that Natalia wished they didn't have to do.

Natalia told their mom what happened at school and asked if it would be okay to go over to Yael's house. Camp—and all the new friends they met there—might have felt like a million miles away, but they had a BFF right here at home.

* * * * *

Way Too Many Body Messages

You've probably heard kids and adults use lots of words to describe their bodies—and maybe yours too. Sometimes those words are kind and loving; sometimes those words are mean and hurtful. You've probably also heard a lot of messages about bodies. Stuff like

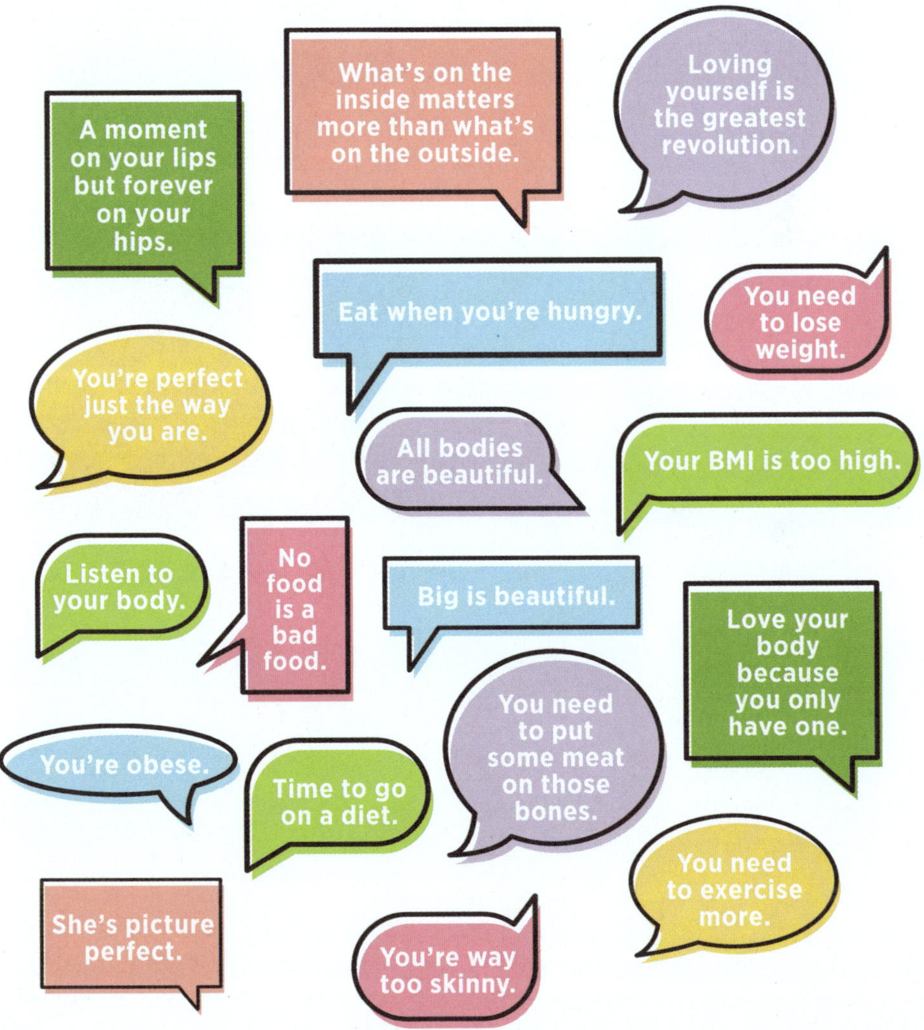

Those messages can be really confusing. Some can be hurtful to yourself or others. Some can make you feel really good or bad, depending on who they are coming from or why someone is saying them. Some are based entirely on misinformation. That's why, in this book, we'll talk about a more compassionate, helpful way to take care of your body and to feel confident about it. We'll meet characters, like Natalia, who are hearing and seeing a lot of the same messages you hear and see every day about bodies and who are learning what to do with them. We'll learn how to keep our bodies healthy and what it means to really love your body, no matter who you are.

CHAPTER 3

MY AMAZING BODY

One morning the boys' camp counselor, Nico, told everyone in the cabin that he had a special adventure planned for them. Gathered between the bunk beds, Troy and his cabinmates whispered excitedly about what the day might bring.

"Do you think we'll take a hike to the lake?" Juan asked.

"Ooh, yeah, maybe we're going fishing!" exclaimed Noah, his hair still tousled from tossing and turning all night in his bunk. Juan knew this was Noah's first time away from his parents, and he was having a hard time getting comfortable at night without his usual bedtime routine and without his Labrador retriever, Scout, at the bottom of his bed.

"Listen up, guys," Nico said, calling everyone to attention. "This morning we're going to be the very first cabin to try out the new ropes course in the forest. It will be super fun, but it will also test your mind and your body. You'll use balance, strength, and coordination to maneuver the ropes. You'll also have to use your minds to focus and to summon all your Camp Corazón bravery. Finally, at the very end of the ropes course, at the highest point, you'll jump out to a bar in front of you and grab onto it. That will take courage, but it will also take what's called **proprioception**—your body's ability to tell where it is in space. Proprioception uses your eyes, your brain, and part of your inner ear to help you balance and to help you not feel dizzy. It's super cool. Oh, and don't worry—you'll be strapped in with a harness and a helmet the whole time. You'll be totally safe, even if you don't feel like it the *whole* time."

Noah, Troy, and Juan all looked at each other, grinning. They felt excited and nervous all at the same time.

The part Troy loved most about Camp Corazón was all the new activities he got to try.

"Okay, Nico!" Troy announced. "Let's do this."

* * * * *

You Are Unique

Being body confident starts with understanding how totally amazing and unique your body is. Did you know that your body is one of a kind? That's right. No one in the entire world has the same body as you do. From the top of your head to the tips of your toes, from the wiring in your brain to the cells in your muscles, down to your fingertips, your body is different from others'. And even though sometimes, as you're growing up, being unique is the *last* thing you want to do (being just like everyone seems so much cooler and safer), it is something to be proud of. Your body also works hard for you every day. That's something to be grateful for. We all have different bodies, different minds, different personalities, and different ways of seeing the world. Some of us wear glasses. Some of us have braces. Some of us have curly hair. Some of us are short and some of us are tall. That's what makes us special—and what makes our world more exciting. The more you understand how completely cool your body is, the more you'll appreciate all it does for you every day.

Your Body Is Super Cool

We all have certain parts of our body that make us smile when we think about them or when we catch ourselves in the mirror. Maybe you love the little dimple you see when you smile or the way your hair falls on your forehead just so. Or maybe you just can't get enough of how your legs let you kick the soccer ball fast down the field or how your heart beats fast when you ride your bike around the neighborhood.

Here are some other totally amazing things about your body you may not realize.

Super Bone Strength

Did you know that our bones are stronger than steel? Even though they might not look like it, our bones are super strong and can support our whole body!

Mighty Heart Pumping

Your heart beats around 100,000 times every day, pumping blood to every part of your body.

Amazing Brain Power

Your brain has about 86 billion nerve cells, helping you think, learn, and do all the cool stuff you enjoy.

Fantastic Healing Powers

If you get a small cut or scrape, your skin can heal itself! It creates a protective cover, and before you know it, it's as good as new.

Muscle Flexibility

You have more than 600 muscles in your body, helping you move, run, play, and do all your favorite activities.

Awesome DNA Code

Your body has a special code called **DNA,** like a supersecret instruction manual! It contains all the information that makes you unique, from the color of your eyes to the way you laugh.

Cool Blinking Reflex

On average, you blink about 15 to 20 times per minute, giving your eyes little refreshing breaks throughout the day.

Unique Fingerprints

Your fingerprints are one of a kind. Even though there are billions of people on Earth, no one else has the same fingerprints as you. It's like having a built-in personal signature!

My Turn | Be a Body Detective

Time to play detective. Find out 4 more amazing facts about the human body. You can ask an adult (like a teacher or your parent), use the internet (ask an adult to supervise), or find facts in a book about the body you have at home (or that you check out at the library).

List the body facts you find here.
1.
2.
3.
4.

You Are More Than Just a Body

The month after camp ended, Hayley started back at school. At camp, surrounded by her new besties, it seemed like her looks didn't matter much. People there told her she was funny. They laughed at her impersonation of the camp director and at her silly dance moves. But back home in Michigan, people seemed to care about her appearance. They focused on her looks EVERY. SINGLE. DAY. It was cringe because, well, what if she didn't stay that way? There was so much pressure to stay exactly how she was.

"Sweetie, don't eat too much. You want to keep that girlish figure!" her mom said.

"Is that a zit!?!?!" her older brother said. "Uh-oh. Better cover it up!"

"Hayley, your legs look long and lean. Perfect form," her gymnastics coach told her.

"Looks matter," her older sister told her.

Sometimes, Hayley worried that if her skin and body weren't perfect, she wouldn't be the kind of person anyone wanted to be around.

All that talk about her looks—and about what they'll get her—was too much. And even if she weren't in the fourth grade with new pimples and hair in odd places (and what was that smell in her armpits?!), it felt like a lot of pressure to be perfect. Plus, she felt weird with adults telling her she should look a certain way so that people will like her—especially boys. Wasn't liking herself enough? Why did everyone else have to like her too?

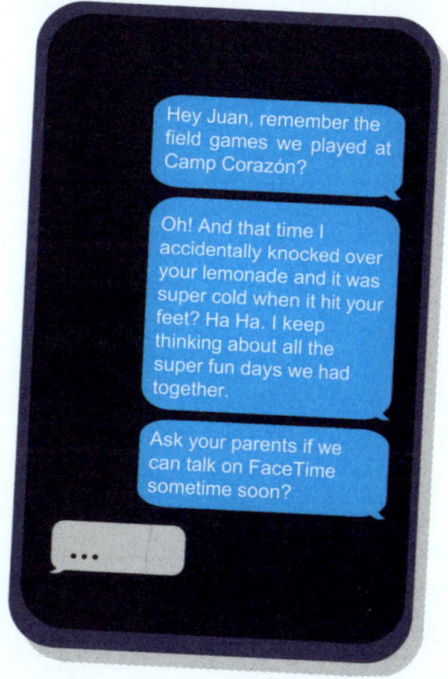

Hayley thought back to how, at camp, she used her body to do all kinds of cool things, like the ropes course. She used her mind and heart to do even more incredible things, though, like make forever friends. And she suddenly wanted to remind herself about all those other, way more important parts of who she was. She thought about who made her feel great about all the parts of herself at school (her friend June, for sure!) and how she could keep in touch with all her forever friends from camp too.

* * * * *

Your Body Is One Small Part of Who You Are

It makes sense that Hayley felt uncomfortable when people focused only on her looks. That's because her looks are only a little part of what makes her *Hayley.*

Just like Hayley, you are so much more than your physical appearance. Just think of all the wonderful parts that make up who you are—parts that are much more important than how you look. The way your brain works, the way you treat your friends with kindness, the things that make you feel happy inside (like learning new facts, spending time with your friends, or an activity you do after school), and your family culture all matter *a lot.*

My Turn | What Makes Me Special

Take a minute and think about yourself. You are more than your physical appearance.

Write down what's special about each of these for you.
The Way I Think:
The Way I'm a Good Friend:
The Way I Solve Problems:
The Place I'm From (My Heritage or Ethnicity):
The Way I Help My Community:

The Way I Love Other People:
The Way I Help My Family:
The Way My Mind Works:
The Special Things I'm Naturally Good At:
Other Special Things About Me:

Your Changing Body

Your body is constantly changing. Look at all the different ways, every single day, it's transformed over and over.

Red Blood Cells

Your **red blood cells (RBCs)** carry oxygen to all parts of your body, so you can play, run, and have lots of fun. Inside your bones is a special factory called the **bone marrow.** This is where new RBCs are made and where stem cells live. Stem cells are like the trainees learning to become full-fledged RBCs. As these stem cells grow up, they go through special training to become excellent oxygen carriers and join other RBCs in your body. The new RBCs zoom through your bloodstream, picking up oxygen from your lungs and delivering it to all the different parts of your body that need it. Each RBC gets to do its job in the body for about 120 days. After that, they take a break, and new ones come in to continue the important mission of delivering oxygen to every organ you have.

Hair Follicles

Just like plants have roots in the soil, your hair has roots in your scalp. These roots are called **hair follicles,** and they're like tiny, invisible pots in your skin. Your hair goes through different phases. The first phase is the growing phase, where the hair strand is actively growing from its root. After some time, the hair enters a resting phase. It's like the plant taking a little break and not growing for a while. Eventually, the old hair strand might fall out, just like leaves falling off trees in autumn. This is normal, and it makes room for new hair to grow. Once the old hair falls out, a new hair strand starts growing from the same root. It's like a new plant sprouting in your garden.

Just like there are all kinds of plants, there are also all kinds of hair and ways to style it. You might have curly hair, while your friend has straight hair. You might wear your hair under a burka, or in braids, or cropped short on one side. Different hair textures and styles can represent different cultures, individual identities, and ethnicities and are a way to celebrate how unique you are!

Skin Cells

Your skin, which is like a super-protective armor for your body, is always renewing itself. The top layer, the **epidermis,** is shedding old skin cells all the time. Underneath the shedding layer, there are new skin cells waiting to take their place. It's like having a team of little builders ready to replace the old with the new. When you get a cut or scrape, your skin sends special cells to the rescue to fix the damaged area. It's like your skin's repair team working to patch up any holes in the armor. You might notice a scab forming over a cut (imagine a whole army of skin cells crawling to the rescue—it's kinda gross, but kinda cool too!). This is like a natural bandage your body creates to protect the healing area. Underneath the scab, the skin cells are busy rebuilding and fixing things up. As time goes by, the scab falls off, revealing new skin underneath.

Puberty Changes

As you grow year after year, your body also changes in bigger, more noticeable ways, especially during **puberty,** when a person starts changing from a kid into a teenager and, eventually, into an adult. Puberty can make you feel sometimes like you're living in someone else's body entirely, even though it's a natural and gradual process your body goes through as you grow.

In this book, we say **female** when we are talking about people who were born with a **vulva** (the area between their legs that includes the labia, vagina opening, urethra opening, and clitoris) and who usually have ovaries, a uterus, and certain genetics. These people are called *girls* at birth.

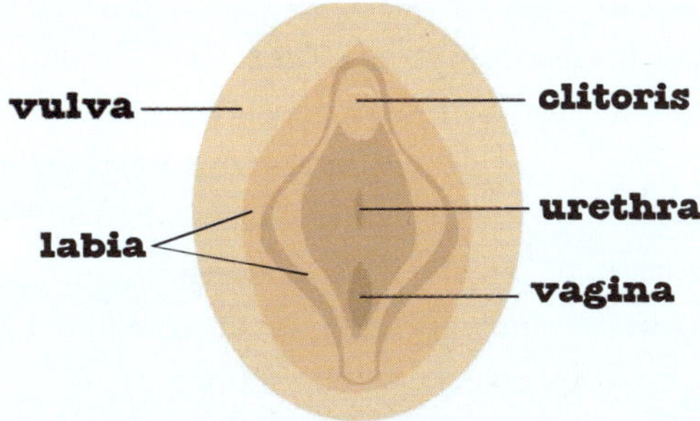

When we say **male,** we are talking about people who are born with a penis between their legs. People who are male generally also have testicles and certain genetics. These people are called *boys* at birth. The label you were given at birth based on the body parts you have is called your **sex assigned at birth.**

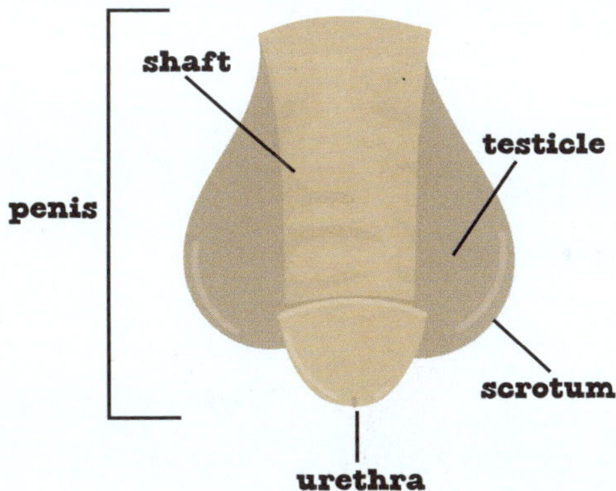

Sometimes, a person's body (the inside parts or outside parts) doesn't fit into the typical male or female category. This is rare but can happen for a number of reasons related to genes or hormones or to changes that happen in development before being born. It is called **intersex.**

Gender identity is what you feel and know you are—boy, girl, neither, or both—regardless of what body parts you have. Many people who are assigned the label "girl" at birth also feel like a girl on the inside; however, some do not. And some people who are assigned the label "boy" at birth don't feel a connection to being a boy. If your gender identity lines up with the sex you were assigned at birth, that's called being **cisgender.** If your gender identity doesn't line up with the sex you were assigned at birth, that's called being **transgender.**

Puberty starts at different times for everyone. For females, puberty usually begins between the ages of 8 and 13. For males, puberty usually begins between the ages of 9 and 14. Puberty takes a long time, and often it can feel like it's taking longer than you want it to (or longer than it's taking for your friends). It lasts for about 5 years. During puberty, all kids experience multiple **growth spurts** (fast jumps in height), body changes, and plenty of mood swings. That's because **hormones** (chemicals in our bodies that travel through our bloodstream and deliver important messages to different parts of the body) shift as you're changing from a child to an adult. Those changes will make your body look and feel different. And even though it can be a little confusing (or sometimes even scary), they're all supposed to happen.

Genitals are the body parts between your legs.

These Changes Happen to Every Body During Puberty

Growing Taller

During puberty, your body releases a hormone called **growth hormone** that stimulates the part of your bones responsible for making you taller.

Skin Changes and Body Odor

You may notice more oiliness or pimples, plus a stronger smell in your armpits and the rest of your body, as you go through puberty because of hormone changes.

Body Hair

Other hormones called **androgens** (including one called **testosterone**) lead to more body hair in areas like your underarms and your **pubic area** (the part of your body between your legs where your vulva or penis and scrotum are).

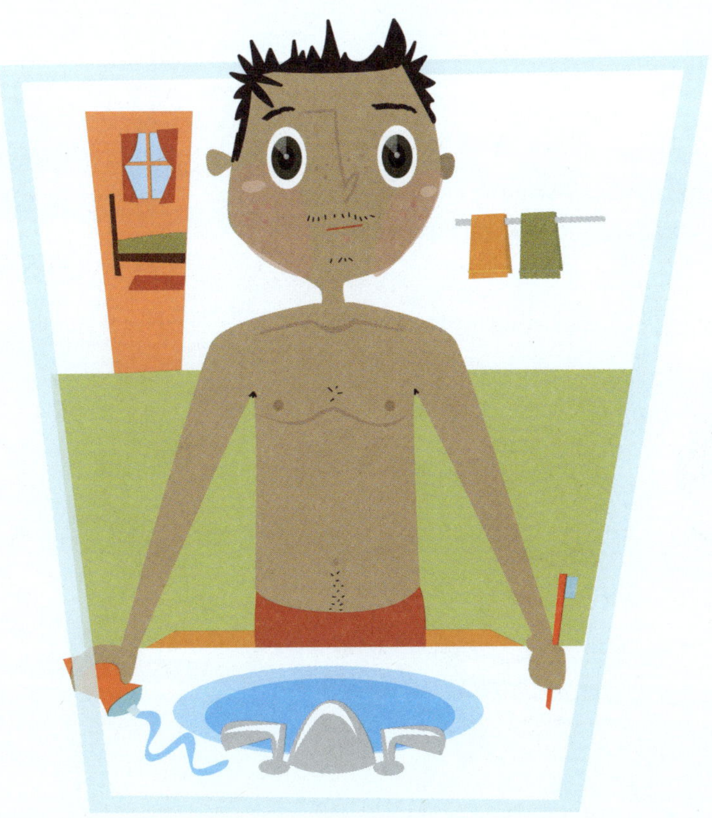

Emotional Rollercoaster

Hormones also influence emotions during puberty. You may have more mood swings than you're used to or experience new emotions you haven't felt before as your body changes.

These Changes Happen to Females During Puberty

Breast Development

Other hormones (**estrogen** and progesterone) make the tissue in your chest area develop and breasts start to emerge.

Hip Widening

Estrogen also makes your hips widen and changes the bones in your pelvis.

Menstruation (Period)

Hormones are also responsible for females eventually having a period. A **period** (or **menstruation**) is when your body sheds the lining of your uterus (the inner part of your reproductive system).

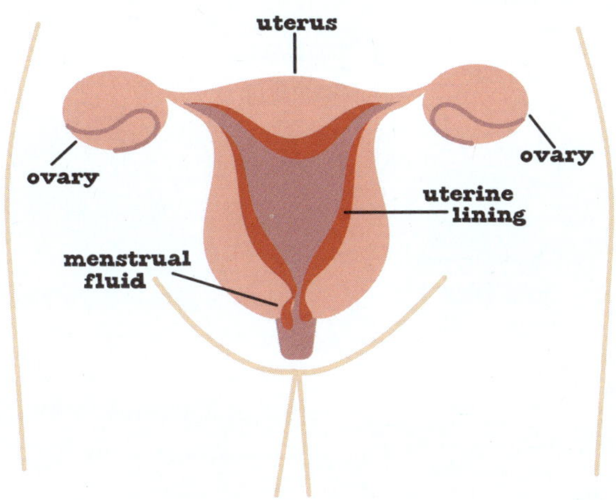

These Changes Happen to Males During Puberty

Chest and Shoulder Broadening

Hormones (especially testosterone) contribute to muscles developing in the chest and shoulders. This leads to a broader and more defined upper body as you grow.

Genital Growth

Hormones cause the genitalia to grow. This includes the penis getting larger, as well as the testicles.

Voice Deepening

During puberty, hormones cause the vocal cords to grow, leading to a deeper voice. Males may also hear fluctuations in their voices during puberty.

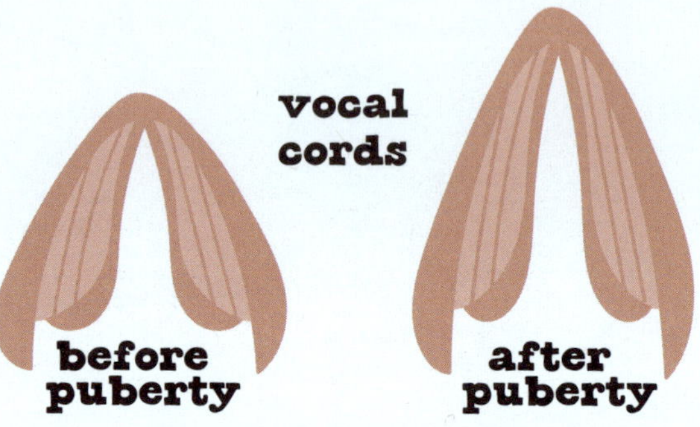

Muscle Development

Testosterone plays a significant role in the development of muscles. As you go through puberty, you may notice your muscles become bigger and stronger, especially if you're active or you participate in sports.

My Turn | Signs That Puberty Has Started

Remember, everybody goes through puberty at a different pace, and not all puberty changes happen at the same time. Place a check mark in the column that matches your experience so far with changing body parts.

	Changes I Have Noticed			
Body Part	**✓ Not Yet**	**✓ A Little**	**✓ A Lot**	**✓ Not Sure**
Breasts/Chest				
Stomach				
Thighs				
Hips				
Hair				
Genitals				
Muscles				
Skin				
Emotions				

Sometimes kids think they're not going through puberty fast enough or that they're going through it too early. The reality is that all bodies go through puberty at different times, and being late or early to puberty is pretty rare. If you're worried that puberty isn't "on time" for you, talk to your pediatrician. We get questions about puberty all the time, and we want to hear yours!

What to Love About Your Body

No matter what body parts you have and how your body is changing (or not changing yet!), your body is doing amazing things for you every single moment of every single day—pumping blood, thinking, digesting, and feeling.

Part of loving our bodies is celebrating them and remembering to be grateful for them.

Practice standing in front of a mirror and being kind to all the amazing, unique parts of your body. Pick one part of your physical body you want to be kind to. Tell it why you're grateful for it. For example, "I'm grateful for my legs because they help me to run fast!"

My Turn | Thanking My Body

Your body helps you do so many amazing things every day. Let's show some love to the following body parts as you think about why you are thankful for each one.

Write down why you're grateful for the following body parts:	
Eyes	
Ears	
Nose	
Mouth	
Hair	
Arms	
Legs	

Stomach	
Lungs	
Heart	
Feet	
Hands	
Other	

When You Hear Other People Being Negative About Their Bodies

Hayley was in the bathroom grabbing a hairbrush when she heard her mom sigh from the shower. "Yuck, this tummy just will not get flatter."

Hayley stopped, surprised. "Huh?" she called. "Mom, is that you?"

"Grab me a towel, honey, I don't want you to have to see this fat body." Her mom reached around the glass door, extending her hand.

Hayley never liked it when her mom called herself fat around her. She thought she was beautiful just the way she was. Should she tell her to stop? Should she agree? Hayley's homeroom teacher had been teaching a new unit called "All Bodies Are Beautiful." Everyone her age seemed to understand that being mean to your body was a bad thing. So why was her mom talking to herself that way?

* * * * *

Many of the adults in your life may not have gotten the chance to learn about loving their bodies in the same way you are learning to do right now. Most kids today still face a lot of body negativity in the world, but body negativity used to be *even more acceptable* in the past. In fact, just a few generations ago, no one thought much about using unkind words to talk about different body types. The way genes influence our bodies' shape and look—from the features of our noses, to the size of our feet, to our skin type—was poorly understood by most people. They also didn't know that focusing too much on just your body (instead of on the way your mind works or how great of a friend you are) was harmful for us. They weren't taught that their unique, awkward, amazing bodies deserved to be celebrated, not criticized. A lot of adults in your life are just now learning how the way we talk and think about our bodies influences how we feel about them—just like you are learning!

You Can Be a Body Positivity Advocate

Here's the good news! The world is changing to be more accepting of all body types and to be more aware of body negativity and positivity. Kids like you can help change how the whole world talks about loving our bodies. You can be a **body positivity advocate**—someone who stands up for others and for yourself when it comes to loving the bodies we're in!

You're not responsible for making other people feel good in their own bodies, but if you hear someone talk negatively about their body, it's okay to say something. For example, if a friend of yours calls themselves an unkind name, like "ugly," you can say, "Hey, no one calls my friend a mean name." If your parent or sibling talks about their body negatively, it's okay for you to speak up then too. You can say, "Ouch! That was harsh!" If you see something that's negative on a show you're watching or in a book you're reading, it's a great idea to call that out too. You can use words like, "That seems unfair," or "That was unkind." The more we have conversations about what we see in the world that doesn't line up with how we want the world to be, the better! Extra bonus: The more we **advocate** (stand up for someone or something) for others, the more practice we'll have advocating for ourselves when people are body negative!

My Turn | Be a Body Positivity Advocate

Being a body positivity advocate means helping the world be more accepting of all the different body types. Start loving your unique body and help others around you to do the same.

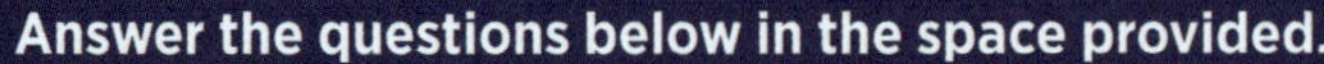

What could you say if you hear an adult, a sibling, or a friend talk negatively about their body?

What could you say to someone to encourage them to use more positive words when they are talking about their body?

Juan stood at the platform way up high in the trees above Camp Corazón, waiting his turn to jump out toward the bar hanging in front of him. He looked back at Troy, who gave him a big thumbs-up. Then he took a deep breath, bent his legs, mustered every ounce of bravery he could find inside himself, and leapt outward into the air, eyes open and arms outstretched. That's when Juan felt his hands grasp the bar and his body swing out below it.

"I did it!" he yelled, proud of what his body could do but also what he just accomplished as a *whole person.* He'd been scared, but he'd also been brave.

Below him, his new friends cheered and clapped as the counselors lowered him slowly to the ground and into a huge group hug.

CHAPTER 4

TAKING CARE OF MY BODY

Greta's favorite part of Camp Corazón was that she felt like a mini adult. Sure, her camp counselor, Molly, made sure everyone in their cabin made it to the mess hall in time for breakfast and that they made it to all the daily preplanned activities, but once it was free time, Greta loved wandering the campgrounds with her cabinmates, Natalia and Bree. Bree and Greta were friends from school and had signed up for camp together. If they were in a creative mood, they moseyed on over to the arts and crafts room. If they wanted to swim, there were lifeguards stationed at the pool.

With all that independence came a lot of responsibility. Molly reminded them each day at their evening meeting about the schedule for the next day and the expectations she had for them when it came to safety. She told them to stay with a buddy, to walk on the main pathways, and to make sure they checked in with the supervisor at the pool towel cart.

"What sounds fun today?" asked Bree, as she stretched out on the top bunk.

"We could go to the archery station," Natalia suggested, grabbing their arm braces.

Bree wrinkled her nose. "Not my thing."

"Ooh, how about ping-pong?" suggested Greta.

"Yes!" they all screamed at once. "Jinx! One, two, three, four, five, six, seven, eight, nine, ten!"

The 3 campers collapsed in a fit of giggles.

"Ping-pong it is!" cried Greta.

* * * * *

Taking Care of Your Body Is a Big Responsibility

Taking care of your body is a big responsibility, but it's also a lot of fun. And it's one of the most important responsibilities you'll have your whole life because your body is the only one you've got! When you were just a baby, your parents were completely responsible for taking care of your body. Their job was to bathe you, feed you, and make sure the place you slept was safe and comfortable. But you've also been taking care of your body since you were very little. Habits like brushing your teeth, washing your hands, taking a bath or shower, and wearing your seat belt all help you stay safe and healthy.

As you grow older, you'll do more and more to take care of your own body. That means you need to learn to give it what it needs to stay healthy and strong for a very long time: plenty of rest, good body hygiene, lots of water, movement, foods that will nourish it and give it energy, and a whole bunch of kindness.

Giving Your Body Rest

Even though you don't need as much sleep as you did when you were a baby or younger kid, you still need a lot (even though it doesn't always feel that way). Making sure to get a good night's sleep helps your body and brain rest so you can have lots of energy during the day to play, learn, and feel your best. Here's the amount of sleep doctors recommend for kids of all ages.

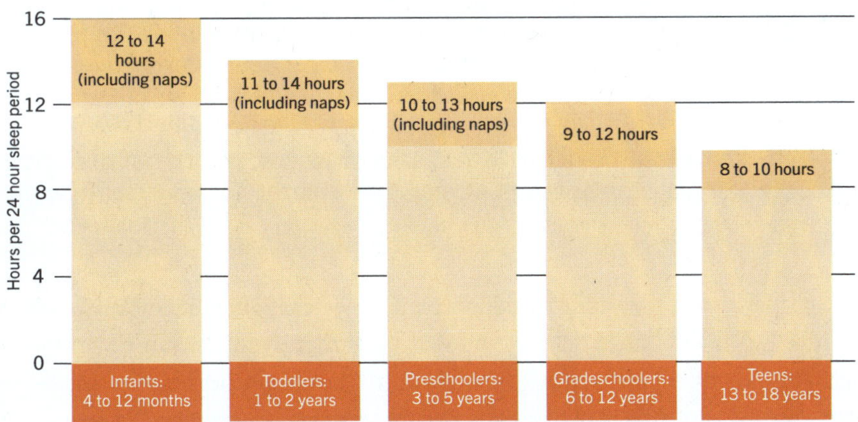

The American Academy of Pediatrics (AAP) has issued a statement of endorsement supporting these guidelines from the American Academy of Sleep Medicine (AASM).

Source: American Academy of Pediatrics. Healthy sleep habits: how many hours does your child need? HealthyChildren.org. Accessed July 3, 2025. https://www.healthychildren.org/English/healthy-living/sleep/Pages/healthy-sleep-habits-how-many-hours-does-your-child-need.aspx and *J Clin Sleep Med*. 2016;12(6):785–786.

As you grow from an infant to an adult, you need less sleep. You may not need as much sleep as a 4-month-old baby, but you still need a lot! To make sure you get enough sleep, pay attention to **sleep hygiene,** the environment you sleep in and the way you prepare your body to fall asleep.

My Turn | Am I Getting the Rest I Need?

For each topic below, circle the face that matches best.
Consistent Bedtime and Wake Time
Screens Off 1 Hour Before Bed
Bedroom Dark and Cool
Getting Enough Hours of Sleep
Putting All Devices in a Room Other Than My Bedroom to Charge
Creating a Sleep Ritual
Resting During the Day

If you got all sad faces, or even just a few sad faces, on this chart, it just means there's an opportunity for you to make some changes to get the rest your body needs. We all have areas where we can improve our health! Review the sleep hygiene tips earlier in this chapter, pay attention to which ones might help you sleep better and wake up more rested, and make some changes. Talk to your parents about how you can make even a few changes to get the rest you need. Your pediatrician can also help your family brainstorm changes you can make to your sleep routine and environment. They're experts in kid sleep, after all!

Here are a few sleep hygiene tips. I know that these recommendations might feel really hard and that some of your friends might not be following these tips, but trust me, your mental health and brain health will thank you for getting better sleep. Here are some ideas that I suggest; try some!

- Try to go to sleep at the same time every night and wake up at the same time every morning, even on the weekends. Set an alarm. By keeping a consistent sleep schedule, your body will be more likely to fall asleep and wake up more easily.
- Turn off all your screens at least 1 hour before you want to fall asleep. It's a good idea to never have screens in your bedroom. This will help

you fall asleep more easily and not be disturbed by alarms or notifications during the night.

- Keep your bedroom dark and cool and make your bed the only place you sleep at night, if possible.
- Create a sleep routine that you repeat every night before bed. Some kids like to read a book, listen to a favorite song, or take a calming shower to let their brains know it's time to rest.

Resting your body also means giving it a break while you're awake by making sure you leave time for having fun in your daily schedule and taking breaks from working while you're at school or doing homework.

Body Hygiene and Maintenance

For the past year, Greta noticed that small **pimples** kept cropping up on her forehead and nose area. Every once in a while, she caught a whiff from her armpits that just did *not* smell right (was that the smell of rotten eggs?!), and then she realized, it was her! (Eww! Gross!) She started using deodorant

and focusing on **body hygiene and maintenance** (keeping yourself clean and cared for). She realized that, even though what she looked like didn't matter as much as who she was on the inside, she felt more confident when she had fewer pimples (pimples are also called **acne** or, sometimes, **zits**) and smelled less like body odor.

All bodies need regular maintenance to stay healthy, especially during puberty. That means taking care of them on a daily basis. Here are a few ways you can keep your body in tip-top shape.

Wash Your Hands

Wash your hands often, especially before eating and after using the bathroom. Trim your nails every few weeks so germs (ahem, like *boogers* if you *happen* to pick your nose) don't get stuck underneath them, making your hands more difficult to clean well. Washing your hands regularly is the best way to prevent illness.

Be Safe

Be careful and use your common sense. Always look left and right before crossing the street. Make sure no cars are coming and use crosswalks if possible. When you're in a car, follow the law by wearing your seat belt and by sitting in the back seat. It helps keep you safe if there's a sudden stop. When you're riding a bike or scooter, always wear a helmet. Helmets protect your head and keep you safe if you fall. Learn your home address and your parents' phone numbers. This helps if you ever get lost or need to call your parents.

Brush Your Teeth

Brush your teeth at least twice a day (in the morning and before bed) and after eating, especially if you have braces. Food can get stuck in the wires, brackets, and bands and make your breath sooooo stinky if you don't remove it! Make sure to brush for about 2 minutes. Floss your teeth every day. It's good to visit the dentist regularly too. Dentists are experts who can help keep your teeth in tip-top shape.

Bathe/Shower Regularly and Use Deodorant

Taking a bath or shower every day keeps us clean, decreases acne, and helps prevent underarm (and other!) odors like Greta experienced. Use a gentle cleanser and water to wash your face once or twice a day. This helps remove dirt and sweat and helps keep your skin clean. Use a moisturizer with no fragrances, dyes, or harsh ingredients to hydrate your skin and maintain your skin barrier. You also need sunscreen with at least 30 SPF every day to protect your skin from the sun's rays, which can be harmful. Remember, not all skin care products are safe for young skin, even if beauty companies advertise them to kids your age. Your pediatrician can help you understand what ingredients are okay to use and create a basic skin care regimen that keeps your face and body safe and healthy. They can also help you if you continue struggling with acne even though you're taking good care of your skin. Using deodorant each morning is also a helpful way to keep you smelling good and feeling confident.

My Turn | How My Body Maintenance Is Going

For each topic below, circle the face that matches best.	
Washing My Hands	😊 🙂 😐 🙁 😞
Being Safe	😊 🙂 😐 🙁 😞
Brushing My Teeth	😊 🙂 😐 🙁 😞
Bathing/Showering Regularly and Using Deodorant	😊 🙂 😐 🙁 😞

A few sad faces on this chart mean you have a chance to improve your health, even if it takes a while to build better body maintenance. Remember, changing habits takes weeks, not days, so don't feel bad if it feels like hard work at first or if you forget to pay attention to body maintenance every now and then. Your parents and your pediatrician can help you brainstorm ways to stay motivated and on track too!

Remember, Every Body Is Different

Natalia has to take special care of their body in unique ways since they spend so much time sitting. Because there's a lot of pressure on their butt from their wheelchair, they can get super sweaty, especially on a hot New York day, so Natalia brings wipes with them to school in a small pouch. They wipe at lunch, right after school before wheeling home, and then again once they reach their little apartment on 6th Avenue.

Natalia also performs specific neck exercises their physical therapist taught them to do before heading to bed at night. Chin to chest, right ear to shoulder, left ear to shoulder, head to back—5 times one direction, then 5 times the opposite way. Rotating their neck helps prevent headaches and helps them relax before drifting off to sleep.

* * * * *

Every body is different. That means you or your friends may have different types of body maintenance they need to do than other people you know. For example, a person with a kidney disorder may need to check their urine every morning for a substance called **protein** to make sure they're not sick. Someone with type 1 **diabetes** will wear an insulin pump and may have to test their blood sugar to make sure it's in the correct range. A person with **attention-deficit/hyperactivity disorder (ADHD)** needs to see their doctor regularly for blood pressure, weight, and medication checks. If you feel comfortable, you can share with others about how your body is unique. It's also okay to keep some of your individual body maintenance needs private, though, if there's no need to share them or if that's your preference.

My Turn | My Individual Body Maintenance Needs

Everyone's body is unique! Think about the ways you take care of your body to make it stronger and healthier.

Write down 3 specific needs you have for taking care of your body.
1.
2.
3.

Understanding your unique body maintenance needs can help you pay attention to them more intentionally. When we understand our special, sometimes complicated, bodies, it helps us know what they need to be super healthy for a lifetime. If you're having trouble understanding how your body works, what it needs for maintenance, or why you have to take certain medications or go to certain types of therapy, ask for help! Your parents, trusted adults at school (like a school nurse or a teacher), and your pediatrician are all there to make taking care of your body as simple and understandable as possible. It's a team effort!

Hydration

Kids live in a world full of energy drinks, protein shakes, caffeine beverages, and meal replacements, but water is *the* best option for keeping your skin hydrated and healthy from the inside out. You need about 6 to 8 cups of water per day. That's because your body is made of so much of it! Your whole body is made of about 60% water.

When you play, run, or even just sit still, your body sweats to cool down. Drinking water helps replace the water you lose when you sweat. Water also helps your body do all the cool stuff it does, like digest food, make energy, and even help your brain think clearly. Water helps your muscles and joints stay flexible and strong. So, when you play sports or run around, drinking water keeps you feeling good and helps your muscles move smoothly. And, finally, water helps your body fight off germs and sickness. It helps your body flush out things it doesn't need, like when you go to the bathroom.

My Turn | Am I Getting the Hydration I Need?

For each topic below, circle the face that matches best.	
Drinking Water When I Wake Up	😊 🙂 😐 😕 ☹️
Drinking Water at Meals	😊 🙂 😐 😕 ☹️
Drinking Water With Snacks	😊 🙂 😐 😕 ☹️
Drinking Water When I Exercise	😊 🙂 😐 😕 ☹️

Hydrating throughout the day can be easier if you make a plan and develop a daily routine. Try drinking a big cup of water right when you wake up and with every meal and snack. Take sips of water when you exercise to keep yourself hydrated too. If water tastes boring to you, try adding a slice of fresh orange, frozen strawberries, or a squeeze of lime. You can also cool it with ice to make it more interesting!

Movement and Nutrient-Rich Foods

Cars need the right kind of fuel to go zooming down the road. Similarly, our bodies need a wide variety of nutrient-rich foods to give us energy, to grow, and to keep us strong. They also need to move often so they run well. We'll talk about these parts of taking care of your body even more in Chapters 6 and 7.

Giving Your Body Love

One of the most important ways you can take care of your body is to speak kindly to it. For example, even though it may feel really silly, telling your legs how grateful you are that they let you run fast in PE. Or tell your brain how impressed you are that it could solve that math equation so early in the morning are both forms of body love. The more you practice giving your body love, the more natural it will feel. Try imagining that you're talking to a friend. At first it feels hard to talk to yourself in your head or out loud.

Speaking kindly to yourself is essential for body love because whatever words you use when you talk about your body are the words you'll believe. If you speak unkindly to yourself day after day, you're more likely to feel bad about yourself. On the other hand, if you speak lovingly to yourself day after day, you're more likely to feel great about who you are. You can use whatever words you like to describe your body, as long as those words are loving.

Taking Care of Your Body Means Building Healthy Habits

Because you only have one body your entire life, consistently taking care of it well is what matters most. That means paying attention every day to what we talk about in this chapter: how you're doing with rest, hydration, body hygiene, nutrient-rich foods, movement, and body celebration.

My Turn | My Body Love Words

Think about how you are grateful for your body.

In the space below write down how your body fits these Body Love Words.	
Amazing	
Special	
Magical	
Unique	
Beautiful	
Strong	
Resilient	
Different	
Healthy	
Sturdy	
Flexible	
Hardworking	
Wonderful	
Other	

My Turn | Taking Care of My Body

How much love do you give your body?

For each topic below, circle the face that matches best.	
Movement	
Nourishment	
Rest	
Hydration	
Maintenance	
Celebration and Kindness	

If you have some work to do on body love, take heart. Sometimes just paying attention to where we can improve can motivate us to make small changes that add up to a lifetime of body love and health. Tell a trusted adult where you are now on the body love chart and where you want to be. You have years and years to work on loving your body—and your body love team (your teachers, your coaches, your parents, and your pediatrician) are here to help!

* * * * *

Bree and Greta jumped up and down.

"Victory!" Natalia proclaimed, resting their paddle on the ping-pong table. "We finally got to 20 back-and-forths without the ball falling off the table."

"I think that's called a volley," Greta answered, laying her head on her arms. "But now that we're all done, I need a shower, a bottle of water, and maybe a snack. Then I'm taking a celebratory nap."

"Whoever makes it back to the cabin fastest gets first dibs on the shower!" yelled Bree, running out of the lodge and down the forest path toward cabin number 16.

"You're on!" Greta and Natalia squealed, taking off after her.

CHAPTER 5

BODY TYPES, BODY SIZE, AND BODY BULLYING

Campers at Camp Corazón had a lot of independence in the afternoons, but in the mornings, they had the chance to learn about topics that interested them. They could take a stars and moon class with Counselor Sydney, a plants of the forest class with Counselor Jed, or a cooking class with the camp's head chef, Mrs Johnson, a woman who laughed while stirring and used phrases like "a pinch of this and a sprinkle of that" when referring to measurements.

"Tell me, what's your favorite?" Mrs Johnson asked as Troy kneaded dough for dinner that night. "Étouffé or jambalaya?"

"Oh, jambalaya for sure," Troy said, his eyes lighting up. "The spicier the better!"

"That's how I know you're from the South like me!" Mrs Johnson laughed back, turning to stir a huge pot of beans.

Troy's family was from New Orleans, and they loooooved to cook. Jambalaya, gumbo, collard greens, shrimp and grits—their motto was, "If there's a reason to make 'em, there's a reason to eat 'em." Music and homemade meals, those are the things that made his family tick and that made his house a home, even if that home was now out in California. He moved out West a few years ago when his parents divorced and his dad got a new job in San Francisco.

Troy grew up in the kitchen with his grandma. She never used a cookbook, or measuring cups for that matter, just like Mrs Johnson. Instead, she taught Troy how to prepare food by memory, tradition, and taste. The only thing his grandma loved more than cooking was the New Orleans football team. "Who dat!" she'd yell whenever they scored a touchdown, as she served up fresh beignets—powdered-sugar–coated pastries special to New Orleans.

For Troy and his family, food was love and comfort, so hanging in the kitchen with Mrs Johnson didn't feel like any kind of work at all; it felt like coming home.

* * * * *

Four months later, back in California, Troy was feeling way less at home… or comfortable.

"Why do you look like that?" Olivia said to Troy at school one day. It was just low enough for the principal not to hear. Troy didn't like it.

Troy had always been bigger than most other kids his age, but he never minded when he used to live in New Orleans. Everything there was about good food and good music—and he loved both. He didn't play sports, but he loved to move his body to the beat whenever his favorite songs played and enjoyed walking to school every day. No one seemed too concerned with the size of his body; they cared more about who he was.

Here in California, though, it seemed like it was quite the opposite—everyone liked to talk about how being kind was cool and how all bodies were beautiful, but it seemed like it was all for show. How your body looked mattered more than…*anything?!* This wasn't the first time someone had said something really mean right to his face about how he looked.

Later that day, Troy sat in the exam room at Wellness Pediatrics for his yearly checkup. The nurse had already weighed him, taken his blood pressure, and had him change into a white gown with little blue dots all over it. Now he was sitting on the exam table and, even though they probably didn't mean for him to, he could hear his doctor and his dad talk about him in the hallway.

"We need to draw labs to check for diabetes and high cholesterol," he heard Dr Charles say. "Depending on the results of the labs, we'll decide if we need the help of a specialist, like a dietitian."

All Troy could think was, *Is there something seriously wrong with me?*

Troy was scared. He hated needles, but he hated the thought of being sick even more. Lots of thoughts ran through his mind: *Diabetes? High cholesterol? Dietitian? Did I do something wrong? Is my body bad?*

Soon, Dr Charles and his dad walked back into the exam room.

"How's it going at school?" Dr Charles asked.

That was not the question Troy was expecting. He didn't start with all the scary needle and lab stuff, like he thought Dr Charles would. All the worrisome emotions of the day—what to do about Olivia; the confusion he had about his dad and Dr Charles' hallway talk—came pouring out of him at once.

Troy's eyes filled with tears as he told Dr Charles about how Olivia treated him earlier that day. Dr Charles listened closely as Troy talked and gave him a warm smile.

"Then I heard you talking with my dad just now," he said as he finished his story. "And now I think maybe Olivia was right—my body *is* a joke and it *is* bad. Plus, you mentioned a dietitian. What's that? Does that mean diet? Does that mean I won't get to eat beignets anymore?"

"Troy, keeping our bodies healthy is different for every single person," Dr Charles explained. "You're doing a lot of amazing things right now to stay healthy. You are working hard in school, getting good sleep, keeping your skin healthy, moving your body, and being a great friend. The shape of your body and your size are not what makes someone healthy or unhealthy—or valuable or unvaluable. I'm so glad you told me about this."

Dr Charles pulled out a chair and sat down. "First things first, we have to address what Olivia said to you. What she did is wrong. How she treated you is called bullying. Bullying is when people act purposely mean toward others. Sometimes it can be just once, but sometimes it can be over and over again, which it sounds like has been happening to you. The most important thing for you to know is that you don't ever deserve to be talked to or laughed at that way."

Troy looked down, his eyes filling with tears again, but this time, out of relief. His dad sat down next to him, scooting in close.

"I'm very proud of you for letting us know what's going on at school, Troy," his dad said, placing a hand on his shoulder. "I know that wasn't easy to share."

Dr Charles nodded. "You've already taken the most important step to stop bullying, which was to tell me and your dad about it today. The next thing we'll do is make sure other adults at the school know what's going on so they can put a stop to what Olivia is doing. And, finally, I'm going to give you and your dad some information on how to handle bullying when it happens, like speaking up when you feel safe to do so or going to get help from a trusted adult."

Dr Charles handed Troy a bullying pamphlet and walked him through it step by step. (You'll learn all the steps in "Putting an End to Body Bullying" later in this chapter so you can handle bullies too!) He also took out a brochure from a drawer below the examination table called *Growing Bodies: A Team Approach* that explained more about how dietitians help doctors keep kids safe and healthy. Troy set it down on the table and kept listening.

"Now, let's talk about your body. I want to make sure that every single patient I see is healthy, and that means checking different things for different kids," Dr Charles explained. "Since you live in a bigger body, I want to make sure that certain parts of your body are healthy—your liver, your heart, and the way your body handles sugar. For someone who lives in a thinner body or a really short body, I'd have other labs I might want to check. It's very possible they'll be just fine. And if they are, we'll keep going with working on healthy nutrition and a movement plan that's unique to you, including a few beignets once in a while!"

"If some of the labs come back showing that your body is having a hard time handling sugar or that your liver or heart could be working too hard, we'll get help from a team of people who specialize in those things," Dr Charles continued. "That might include a dietitian. And, if it does, we'll make sure they know all about the spices and flavors you love as we create a plan just for you, including foods that are special to you from back home."

The stress of the day still made Troy tired and overwhelmed, but he felt a little better about the tests Dr Charles might have to do—and a lot better about going to school the next day. When he got home, he knew just who he wanted to talk to. He walked next door to his best friend Jeremy's house. Jeremy and Troy both loved band, and they both saw Dr Charles. Last month, Jeremy told Troy that he had to have blood taken from his arm for something called "anemia." Maybe he could give Troy some tips on what to expect at his next visit.

* * * * *

Health at All Body Sizes

Just like Dr Charles told Troy, the size of your body does not define how healthy you are. You can be healthy or unhealthy at any size. For example, a really thin person *or* a person with a large body who hardly ever moved their body, who only slept 3 hours a night, and who watched television shows all day wouldn't be considered very healthy. On the opposite end of the spectrum, a really thin person *or* a person with a large body who exercised so much they injured themselves, slept all day, or never spent time having fun would also not be considered healthy. Health is not about size—it's about taking good care of yourself!

A Team Approach

Sometimes, taking good care of yourself means working with a team of experts who specialize in different areas of the body. Dr Charles told Troy they might need a team approach depending on Troy's lab results. Here are some of the team members Troy might visit who work specifically on healthy movement, nutrition, heart health, and growth.

Cardiologist: An expert in the human heart and diseases like high cholesterol. **Cholesterol** is a fatty substance in the blood your body needs. If there's too much of it, though, it can be harmful to the heart. This type of expert makes sure your heart is pumping well and delivering blood and oxygen to every part of your body. Your body's cells all need oxygen to work.

Dietitian: An expert in nutrition and the foods humans eat. This type of specialist helps you understand how different foods make your body strong and healthy and how much of each kind of food your body needs. Dietitians can help families make a plan with nutrient-rich foods, no matter what kinds of foods their favorites are. For example, the dietitian Troy will see can make sure to incorporate plenty of the flavors he loves.

Endocrinologist: An expert in hormones (chemicals in our bodies that travel through our bloodstream and deliver important messages to the body). An endocrinologist helps prevent, diagnose, and control diseases like type 1 diabetes and type 2 diabetes, disorders where there is too much sugar in the blood for the body to handle.

Gastroenterologist: An expert in the body parts that make up your gut, like your intestines, stomach, and liver. This type of specialist helps keep your food digesting and your entire gut system working properly, including making sure you poop without any trouble!

Mental health therapist: An expert in navigating and understanding a person's feelings and thoughts. This type of specialist helps you understand the way your mind works and helps you manage your emotions.

Physical therapist: An expert in body movement. This type of specialist helps you understand how to prevent injuries and how to keep your muscles and joints strong and pain free.

BMI Is Only One Vital Sign of Health

Dr Charles didn't mention **body mass index (BMI)** to Troy, but you might hear people in the medical field talk about it, so we'll explain it here. BMI is a combination of your weight and height without any clothes or shoes on. It is a measurement that doctors use as a **vital sign** of your health. A vital sign is something doctors check, like your heartbeat or temperature, to see how your body is doing and if you're healthy. For example, blood pressure is a vital sign used to make sure the heart is pumping blood with the right amount of strength. Pulse oximetry checks to make sure your body is getting enough oxygen to stay healthy and to do all the things you love doing. Temperature measures how hot or cold our bodies are.

For a long time, doctors used BMI as one of the main ways to see if someone was healthy or not. Research has shown on its own, though, BMI doesn't give doctors a full picture of your health because it wasn't originally developed to measure kids who are of different races, sexes, and backgrounds. It was developed to measure white adult men! In fact, there are a lot of people who want to eliminate BMI completely as a vital sign of health because it has such troublesome roots in racism and sexism. **Racism** is when people are treated unfairly because of their skin color or background. **Sexism** is when people think that one sex is more important or more valuable than another sex.

Another problem with BMI is that it has to be considered with all the other vital signs and with a number of other things, like

- Your individual body type: Some people have more muscle than others (from the exercises they do, or just naturally!).
- Your activity level and your nutrition habits: Moving your body and eating plenty of nutrient-rich foods help your body and your brain function be top-notch.
- Your mental health: Your brain and your body are tightly linked. A healthy brain is critical for your overall health.

How to Deal With Body Bullies

Unfortunately, Troy's not the only kid who's been body bullied for living in a larger body. Kids are bullied every day for how they look, whether they live in a big or small body, have pimples, are really tall or really short—the list goes on and on. In fact, research has shown that 1 in 5 elementary school-aged kids gets bullied every day. People bully each other for a lot of different reasons, including feeling bad about themselves, not understanding differences in others, or because they are being bullied too.

Bullying is different than teasing, but sometimes it can be hard to tell the difference between the two. Sometimes, someone will say they're "just teasing," but if that teasing makes you feel bad or uncomfortable, it's not okay.

Good Teasing

Teasing is when friends joke around in a fun way and everyone is laughing and having a good time. It's like when your friend says, "You've got the cutest cherub baby dimples on your cheeks—you must have come from Heaven!" and you both giggle because you know it's just silly. Good teasing should feel lighthearted and kind, not mean or embarrassing.

- 👍 Both people are having fun.
- 👍 It stops if someone says, "Hey, that's not funny."
- 👍 It doesn't make anyone feel bad inside.

Bullying

Bullying is when someone hurts another person on purpose—with words or actions—and keeps doing it even when it's clear that it's not funny. If someone makes fun of the way you look, calls you names, pushes you, or tries to make you feel bad, that's bullying. It's *never okay* to hurt someone on purpose.

- 👎 It makes someone feel sad, scared, or left out.
- 👎 It doesn't stop when you ask them to.
- 👎 It happens over and over.

Putting an End to Body Bullying

If you've been bullied about the way your body looks (or for any other reason), here are some steps you can take to stop it.

In the Moment

- Speak up if you feel safe to do so. Look the person in the eye and firmly tell them to stop in a calm, clear voice. If humor comes naturally to you, try laughing it off—it might throw them off guard.
- Walk away if needed. If standing up for yourself feels too hard, uncomfortable, or unsafe, remove yourself from the situation. Don't engage or fight back—find a trusted adult who can step in and address the issue.

Staying Safe in the Future

- Talk to someone you trust. Share what's happening with a parent, a teacher, your doctor, or a counselor—they can help you come up with a plan.
- Stick with others. Bullying is less likely to occur when you're around friends or in spaces where adults are present.

* * * * *

Troy and his dad talked more on their way home about the visit with Dr Charles and about getting a plan in place to stop the bullying.

"You can tell me or ask me anything, anytime, Troy," his dad said.

Later that night, Troy's dad cut the vegetables into small squares before popping them into the pan on the stove. His hips swayed gently to the jazz music playing over their wireless speaker as he poured love into the food he created.

Troy thought back to the other campers in Mrs Johnson's Camp Corazón cooking class 4 months ago. No one else in the class had seemed to care much about the food as they checked off all their mini chef tasks: chopping onions, peeling oranges, and plating cheese trays. They'd chatted with each other about the previous night's campfire ghost story and traded ideas for the next evening's talent show. But not Troy. He'd breathed in the feeling of home and smiled as he thought about how much food was a part of his culture, a part of his family, and a part of who he was.

"Dad?" he whispered, looking over at his father. "Was what Dr Charles said true?"

"Which part, son?" his father replied, turning toward him.

"The part about every body size can be healthy and everyone is different. And that all this testing and stuff doesn't mean I can't, you know, enjoy being me?"

His dad nodded. “Every last word of it. That’s why we love Dr Charles. And Troy, you being *you* is exactly why I love you so much.”

Troy took a deep breath and smiled at his dad. He yelled the New Orleans football chant as loud as he could, shaking his fist and feeling his whole body relax. “Who dat!”

CHAPTER 6

FUELING MY BODY

The Camp Corazón garden was the crown jewel of the entire 100-acre property. Neat rows of tomatoes, kale, spinach, and zucchini grew in wooden planter boxes, just waiting to be plucked when they reached their peak level of flavor. Campers like Greta chose gardening as their daily morning class to learn about soil nutrients, growing techniques, and keeping harmful pests from ruining the camp's harvests.

Mrs Johnson planned the weekly menu based on what was most in season. Peaches from a neighboring farm graced their plates at most dinners, as well as parsley and mint grown in a special box nearest to the kitchen for easy access. Campers found bell peppers and homegrown onions at the daily breakfast omelet station, plus fresh celery and carrot sticks at lunch.

Even if they liked learning about the science of plants, eating nutrient-rich foods was something some campers weren't used to. It took Greta a few days of camp to try more foods than she ate at home—and to realize how delicious those natural treats were. It helped that a lot of her fellow campers were eating foods she'd never tried. That made Greta feel brave! Once she got home, though, it was harder to remember.

It was a few weeks after camp ended. "Daaaaaad!" Greta yelled from the kitchen. "I'm going to have this cinnamon roll, okay? Dad? Are you listening to me? I'm putting it in my mouth right now!"

She could hear her dad's footsteps at the top of the stairs.

"What are you yelling about, honey?" her dad said, appearing at the kitchen door with a basket of laundry.

"I've been trying to tell you for 30 minutes that I want to eat this pastry, but you're not listening, so I just went ahead and ate it," Greta said.

Greta's dad set the laundry basket down. "I was gone for 2 seconds, not 30 minutes. And no, cinnamon rolls are not an option right now. We're about to have dinner. You know the rules—we have fruits and veggies in the refrigerator if you're hungry before a meal."

Tears of frustration welled up in Greta's eyes. "But Dad, there's nothing wrong with cinnamon rolls. Why are you being so mean?"

She turned and stomped around the corner, flopped on the couch, and curled herself into a little ball. "You always say no food is a bad food. Plus, I'm a baker; cinnamon rolls are my life!"

She snapped a mental picture of her creations so she could tell Natalia about them next time they talked.

* * * * *

Nutrients

Is Greta right? Are there no bad foods? Here's the truth.

All foods have **nutrients** (a substance the body needs to function properly), but not all foods are alike, and not all foods have the same type of quality of nutrients. Plus, your body doesn't just need one type of nutrient; it needs a whole lot of different ones to work well.

Imagine your body is like a super-cool car, and nutrients are like the special fuels, oils, gadgets, and gears that the car needs to run smoothly. Just like a car needs different types of fuels and fluids to go fast and stay in great shape, your body needs a variety of nutrients to work properly and stay healthy.

Proteins

Proteins are like the car's strong and sturdy frame. They're a special type of fuel that helps build and repair your muscles and bones, making your body strong and ready for action. You can also think of proteins as the muscles of your body. Proteins are the building blocks of tissues, muscles, organs, enzymes, hormones, and the immune system. Here are some examples of protein:

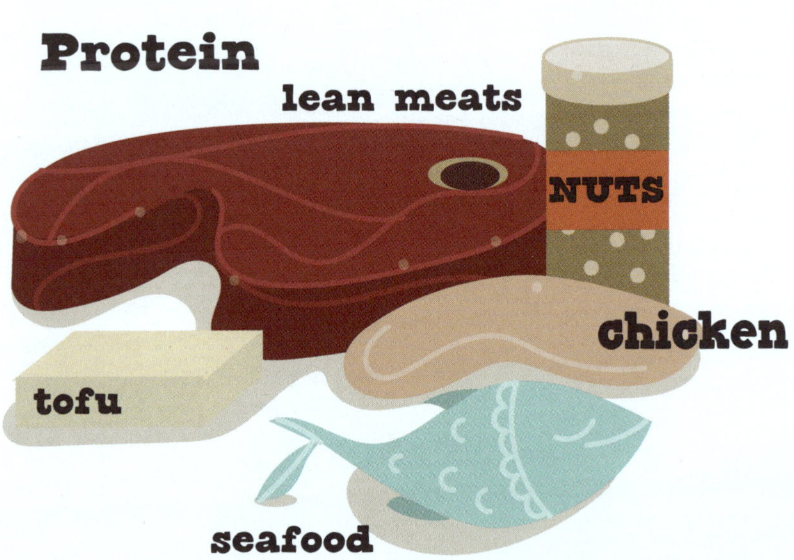

Carbohydrates

Carbohydrates are like the car's fuel. They give your body the energy it needs to play, run, and engage in all the fun stuff. It's like filling up your car with gas before a long drive. **Carbohydrates** give us energy quickly but don't last long in our bloodstream before they get taken up by the body to be used and stored. Here are some examples of healthy carbohydrates:

Fats

Fats are like the oil that keeps the car's engine running smoothly. Fats help your body absorb important vitamins and keep your skin nice and soft. You can also think of fat as the body's energy storage system. It makes sure that, even if you haven't eaten in a while, your body still has some energy. Here are some examples of healthy fats:

Vitamins and Minerals

Vitamins and minerals are like the special gadgets and tools in the car. Each vitamin and mineral has a unique job, just like gadgets in a car. They help your body do things like healing cuts, fighting off sickness, and keeping your teeth and bones strong. Experts call vitamins and minerals **micronutrients** because the body needs smaller amounts of them compared with carbohydrates, proteins, and fats (called **macronutrients**). Even though our bodies don't need as many of these micronutrients to function, they're still totally important for growth, development, and overall health.

Vitamins are nutrients that are critical for normal **metabolism** (the breakdown of food into energy for the body), growth, and development.

Minerals are elements that the body needs for different processes, like making our muscles and nerves work.

Vitamins and minerals are in a lot of the foods we eat naturally. For example, milk, almonds, and some beans have calcium. Meat and dark, leafy greens like spinach have iron. Bananas, oranges, and broccoli have potassium. Salmon, tuna, and eggs all contain phosphorous. The more often you eat different foods, the more micronutrients you can give your body.

So, just like a car needs a mix of fuels, oils, gadgets, and gears to be the best car it can be, your body needs a mix of nutrients to be the healthiest and happiest body it can be! Eating lots of different foods gives your body all the special things it needs to run smoothly so that you feel healthy and strong.

Superfoods

Food can literally give our body superpowers. And while Greta is right that no food is bad, some foods are more powerful than others. These superfoods can help your body fight off infection, keep your eyes and muscles strong, help you stay full, and give you the energy you need to play and learn. Fruits and vegetables, and foods with fiber and protein, are some of the most powerful foods for your body.

Fruits and Vegetables

Fruits and vegetables have lots of antioxidants, vitamins, and phytochemicals. **Antioxidants** are like bodyguards for our **cells** (the tons of little compartments that make up our bodies). They help protect our cells from damage caused by harmful substances called **free radicals.** Just like how bodyguards keep people safe, antioxidants keep our cells healthy and functioning properly. For example, berries are chock-full of antioxidants! Some vitamins and minerals, like vitamin E, vitamin C, and the minerals copper, zinc, and selenium, are antioxidants (and do a lot of other things to help our body). Eating foods that are high in antioxidants, like fruits and vegetables, can help keep our bodies protected from harm. **Phytochemicals** are super-healthy plant chemicals that help protect us from getting sick from diseases like cancer, heart disease, and diabetes.

Try to eat at least 5 fruits and vegetables each day so you get all the nutrients you need to grow. A mix of red, orange, yellow, and green fruits and vegetables offers a wide variety of these powerhouses full of vitamins, antioxidants, and phytochemicals!

Fiber

Fiber is a type of carbohydrate that our body can't digest. It moves through our digestive tracks without getting broken down into sugar like other carbohydrates do. Because it can't be digested, it helps move all the other food through our bodies and keeps the digestive system running smoothly. Fiber can help prevent hard poops and can make sure we poop regularly. It can also slow down how fast sugar gets taken up in the bloodstream, which makes us feel fuller for longer after we eat. Fiber also feeds the good bacteria in our guts, which helps our immune system work like it's supposed to. You can find fiber in fruits, vegetables, whole grains, nuts, seeds, and legumes. To get more fiber in your diet, choose whole-grain breads, pasta, sweet potatoes, and brown rice over white foods like pasta, potatoes, and white rice whenever you can. Eating dark, leafy vegetables also helps you get enough fiber in your diet.

Calcium

Calcium is an important mineral that makes it possible for your bones to grow—something that happens the whole time you're a kid but occurs a lot more during puberty. You need 4 to 5 servings of calcium-rich foods, like dairy products (cheese, milk, and yogurt), leafy green vegetables, and/or soy products to meet your daily calcium needs. Some calcium-rich foods like yogurt also have **probiotics**—good bacteria that can help your body fight some infections. And yes! Ice cream has calcium too. Just make sure this treat isn't the only source of calcium you get because it also has a lot of sugar.

Protein

You need 2 to 3 servings of protein each day. Healthy sources of protein include lean meats (like lean cuts of beef and pork, fish, and chicken). Nut butters, tofu, soy milk, low-fat dairy, beans, and nuts are also great ways to get protein during the day.

My Turn | My Favorite Superfoods

Write down 3 of your favorite foods in each superfood category.

Vegetables	Fruits	Protein	Fiber	Calcium

Draw a line to match the foods with their superpowers.

Berries	Protein
Fish	Calcium and Probiotics
Dark, Leafy Greens	Plant Protein and Healthy Fat
Nuts Like Hazelnuts, Walnuts, Almonds, Pecans	Phytochemicals: Fight Cancer
Yogurt	Antioxidants
Vegetables Like Broccoli, Brussels Sprouts, Cauliflower	Calcium and Fiber

Answers: Berries: Antioxidants; Fish: Protein; Dark, Leafy Greens: Calcium and Fiber; Nuts: Plant Protein and Healthy Fat; Yogurt: Calcium and Probiotics; Vegetables Like Broccoli, Brussels Sprouts, Cauliflower: Phytochemicals: Fight Cancer.

Don't have any superfoods you like? That's okay! Try adding in just 1 or 2 foods to your meals each week. Sometimes it takes trying foods we aren't used to a lot of times before our body decides to like them. You can also ask your parents to help you try recipes that use these foods in small amounts. If you're feeling extra adventurous, get in on the cooking fun with them!

Superfood Meals and Snacks for Healthy Kids

Kids need about 3 to 4 meals per day, plus snacks. Keeping yourself fueled between meals and ready for all the activities in your life is a whole lot easier when you already have some favorite snack ideas in mind. Here are some great snack options before and after you move your body on the sports field, on a walk with your family, or with a quick dance session to your favorite song in your bedroom.

Pre-Activity (For Example, Before a Soccer Game)

Think about giving your body quick energy fuel with healthy carbohydrates before you move your body. Most kids find that eating about 30 to 60 minutes before they are active allows enough time for the food to be absorbed and for their stomachs to settle before they get moving.

- Whole-grain crackers
- Dry cereal
- Oatmeal
- Brown rice or whole wheat pasta
- Granola bar
- Sweet potato
- Whole fruit

Post-Activity (For Example, After a Soccer Game)

When you're done being active, your body needs to recover and refuel. Carbohydrates and protein are what the body needs in this period. Try to have a snack within 30 to 60 minutes after you're active so your body can absorb these healthy nutrients easily and recover faster. This type of snack is great for when you're hungry between meals but don't happen to be active too.

- String cheese and fruit
- Smoothie made with fresh fruit and Greek yogurt or milk
- Energy bite made with nut butter and oats
- Chocolate milk
- Turkey and cheese sandwich
- Whole fruit and nut butter
- Greek yogurt and granola
- Hard-boiled egg and fruit

Are There Any Foods to Avoid as a Kid?

Now you know there are some foods more powerful than others, but are there any foods to avoid? Are some foods completely off-limits? Just like some movies and books aren't appropriate for kids, some foods aren't either. These include

Energy Drinks

Energy drinks like Red Bull, Monster Energy, and Rockstar can be harmful to kids because they can contain lots of caffeine, sugar, and chemicals not tested in kids, like guarana and taurine. Energy drinks can make kids feel jittery, make their hearts race, and make sleep more difficult too.

Foods With Lots of Additives

Additives are chemicals that are used to preserve foods to make them last longer on the shelf or make them taste, look, or feel different in our mouths. They include things like food dyes or artificial flavorings. You might see additives listed in foods like packaged crackers, sodas, and candies. Scientists are still researching just how harmful these additives might be for growing kids, but some additives have already been linked to problems with hormones, growth, and development. And remember, just because something is labeled "organic" or "natural" doesn't necessarily make it healthy. Eating a variety of foods (even if some have a few additives) and focusing on foods with a lot of healthy nutrients is what matters most.

Caffeine

You can find caffeine in coffee, soda, some sports drinks, and some types of tea. Doctors don't recommend caffeine for kids younger than 12 years because it can cause problems with sleep, make kids more anxious, make their hearts beat too fast, or give them irritation in their guts. Plus, lots of specialty drinks at the coffee shop don't only have caffeine; they also have a lot of sugar, cream, and whipped cream. They're like a dessert, even though you might not realize it.

What About Eating Treats?

Treats like ice cream, candy, chips, and fries are delicious, there's no question. That's why we all like to eat them! There's nothing wrong with eating fast food, sweets, or other foods that don't fall into the superfoods category sometimes. Eating them all day every day, though, isn't as nourishing for your body. That's because these foods often don't have as many of the really important nutrients that will help your body grow strong and healthy. Make sure you fill your plate first with nutritious foods at most mealtimes and snack times so you don't miss out on what your body needs!

When Food Means More Than Nutrition

Do you ever eat when you're sad or bored? Or celebrate with a special treat on your birthday? Food doesn't just nourish us; it's also a part of being social and of celebrating. There's a big difference, though, between having a special treat on your birthday and eating to soothe yourself. If you find yourself looking to food as a way to feel entertained, feel better, or feel comfortable, it's important to ask yourself what else could make you feel these ways other than food. Moving your body, writing in a journal, or listening to music are all great ways to respond to your feelings in a healthy way.

Greta loves burgers and fries, especially when paired with a strawberry milkshake, after school. Sometimes, after a hard day—like when kids make fun of her for **stimming** (movements or sounds some people, especially those with autism, use to self-soothe or cope with sensory overload) or because she still sucks her fingers and doesn't play soccer at recess—the food makes her feel like home.

Greta's therapist says that's okay, as long as food isn't the only thing that feels like home.

"You won't always have a burger and fries around when you're feeling low," she says. "Sometimes, having a burger and fries feels great, but too many burgers and fries all at once can make you feel tired and can even make your stomach hurt. When you always use food to fill a hole in your heart, it can feel so good in the moment, but then it can make that hole feel even deeper. So, it's good to have it on the menu of tools in your tool belt for feeling good but not have it be the *only* tool in your tool belt."

* * * * *

My Turn | My Feelings Tool Belt

Think about the tools you have in your tool belt that you can use when you want to celebrate or feel better.

In the space below write down things that bring you comfort or make you smile when you're having a hard day.
Salty and sweet treats
Moving or exercise
Reading a book
Painting, drawing, or crafting
Listening to my favorite song
Talking to a friend
Taking a nap
Taking a walk or sitting outside

Eating the Rainbow

Too much of even the *best* thing can be a bad thing. You likely wouldn't read your favorite book 10 times in a row or play the same game with the same friend 10 days in a row. You've got to mix it up! The same goes for food. The healthiest way to eat healthy is to "eat the rainbow." That means eating a variety of different foods from the superfoods categories throughout the week.

My Turn | The Food Rainbow

Follow the instructions below to begin eating your rainbow.

First, think back to what you ate for breakfast, lunch, and dinner yesterday. Color in which of the superfoods you ate at each meal.

Second, place a check mark next to the superfoods that would help balance each meal.

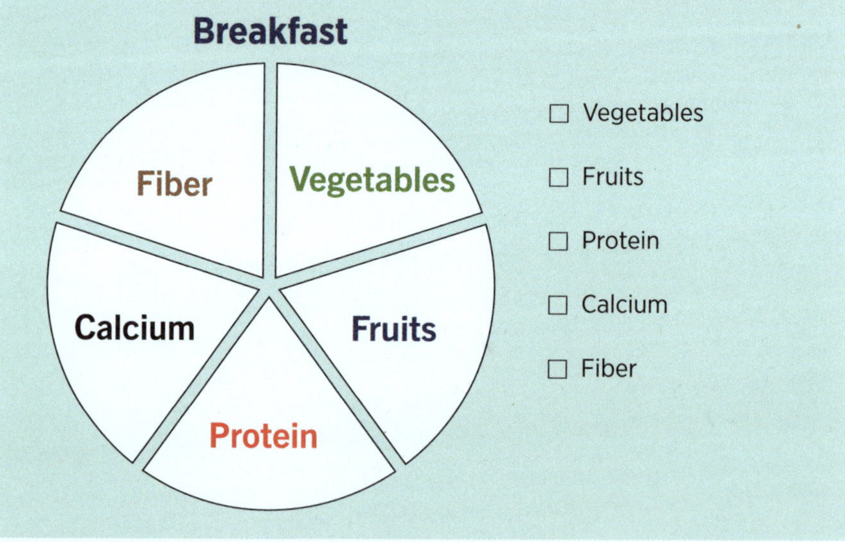

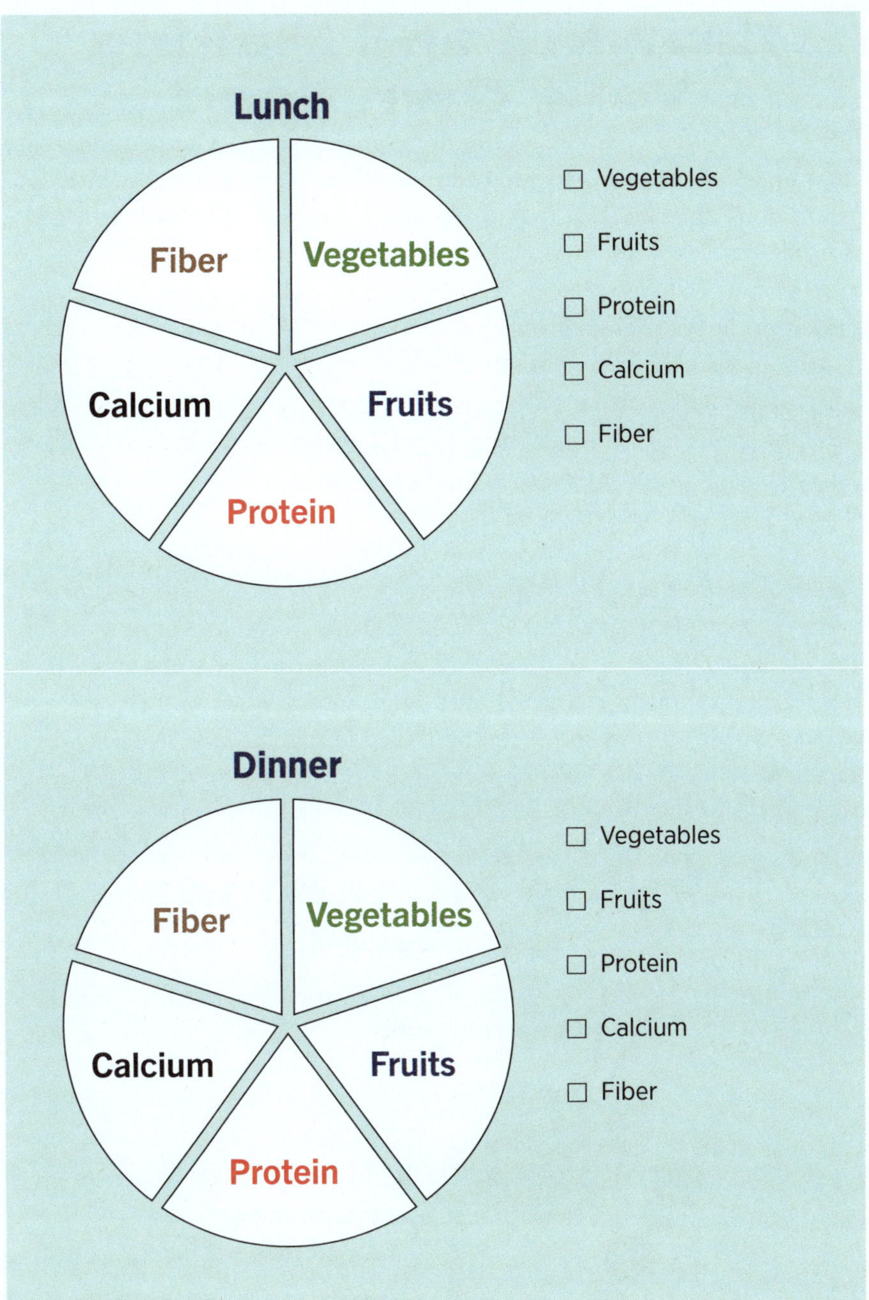
Lunch
Fiber
Vegetables
Calcium
Fruits
Protein
☐ Vegetables
☐ Fruits
☐ Protein
☐ Calcium
☐ Fiber
Dinner
Fiber
Vegetables
Calcium
Fruits
Protein
☐ Vegetables
☐ Fruits
☐ Protein
☐ Calcium
☐ Fiber

Growing and Making Your Own Food

Just like the kids at Camp Corazón discovered, growing a garden is another amazing way to try out new food textures, flavors, and types. Go with your parents to the garden store to pick out which fruits and vegetables you'd like to grow, and make sure to ask plenty of questions about how you'll need to care for your plants so they thrive. It's also fun to try samples of what your garden produces straight from the vine. Somehow, it makes those cherry tomatoes taste even sweeter! Even if you don't have room in your yard for a full garden, you can make a tiny garden in your windowsill with herbs to get in on the gardening action. If these options aren't possible, look for a nearby farmers market or focus on learning about ingredients related to your culture or family as a way to connect to the food you eat.

Helping out in the kitchen will also help you to try new foods. Use a cookbook to look up new recipes you want to try and go with your parents to the grocery store to pick out all the ingredients. You can even get your own kid-safe knife! These make it easier to learn how to chop fruits and veggies and really put you in charge of food prep. Don't forget to clean up after yourself when you cook too. It's normal (and kind of fun!) to make a mess in the kitchen, but it's also important to clean up when you're all done creating.

Trying New Kinds of Food

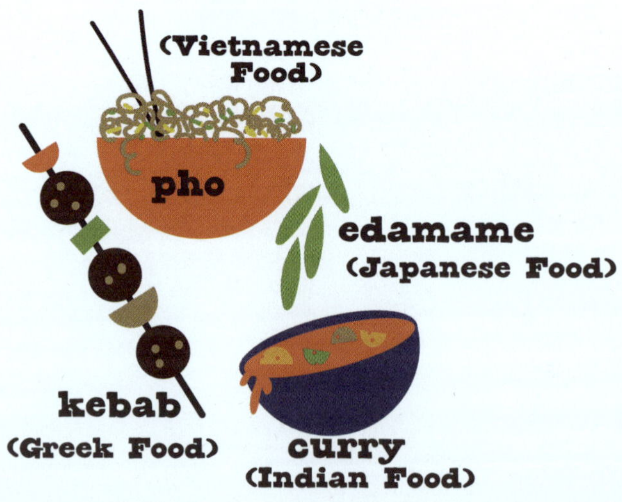

Greta's best friend, Minh Thu, eats completely differently than she does. Minh Thu's family is Vietnamese. When Greta went to Minh Thu's house for dinner, the whole family ate pho, a soup made from clear broth, rice noodles, chicken, and vegetables. It tasted different than the foods she ate at her house—but really good. Every once in a while, Minh Thu brings fresh spring rolls with peanut sauce to school for lunch. They're made of rice paper, wrapped up with shrimp, cilantro, and mint inside. The first time she tried them, Greta wasn't sure if she liked them, but now they are her favorite. In exchange, Greta introduced Minh Thu to aebleskiver, round pancake balls from Denmark you can eat with powdered sugar or apple butter. Minh Thu looked like she was in pure heaven when she tried them.

* * * * *

My Turn | Eating Foods From Around the World

There are so many foods from different cultures, they can't all be listed below. You could go on trying new cuisines for a long time! If you're not sure what foods some of these cultures enjoy, be a food detective! Find out what specialties are served at Russian or Brazilian tables, for example, by looking at books at your local bookstore, library, or online with your parents. You might even find a cool recipe during your search!

Circle the types of food listed below from different cultures (other than yours) that you have tried and liked.

French	Chinese	Thai	Vietnamese
Italian	Creole	German	Russian
Moroccan	Norwegian	Indian	Hawaiian
Mexican	Greek	Canadian	Persian
Spanish	Pakistani	African	Latin American
Brazilian	Cuban	Caribbean	Southern
Japanese	Indonesian	Korean	

Now draw a star next to the types of food from different cultures listed below that you'd like to try but haven't yet.

___ French	___ Chinese	___ Thai	___ Vietnamese
___ Italian	___ Creole	___ German	___ Russian
___ Moroccan	___ Norwegian	___ Indian	___ Hawaiian
___ Mexican	___ Greek	___ Canadian	___ Persian
___ Spanish	___ Pakistani	___ African	___ Latin American
___ Brazilian	___ Cuban	___ Caribbean	___ Southern
___ Japanese	___ Indonesian	___ Korean	

One of the best parts of eating in our international, globally connected world is the fact that we get to try so many different foods all the time. The great news is, it's possible to eat the rainbow no matter where you're from, what your flavor preferences are, or what culture you belong to. The trick is to focus first on filling your plate with lots of fresh superfoods and then to add in a variety of foods from the rainbow. When you and your family go out to eat or when you're invited to a party where there's food you've never had, be brave and try something new! Exploring a friend's food from their culture or sharing your own traditions is all part of the fun!

Greta noticed last week that one of her dads doesn't eat the same foods as the rest of the family at dinnertime. While Greta and her other dad dug in on lasagna, salad, and garlic bread, he drank something called a power smoothie with kale, almond milk, and chia seeds. She had also seen him eat an energy bar for breakfast and a celery stick with peanut butter for lunch. He said his new diet was worth it because, in just 3 short weeks, he'd gone down a couple of sizes. "I'm hungry, but I'm not stopping the diet anytime soon."

* * * * *

Similar to Greta's dad, you might hear the adults in your life talk about new food plans they're trying or about limiting the amount of foods they eat so they can lose weight even if they don't feel full at the end of meals. Just like a lot of adults are still learning how to love their bodies by speaking kindly to them, many are also learning to look at food as fuel and at exercise as a way to be healthy and happy, instead of trying to achieve a certain size. If you're hungry, you should eat! If you don't, your body and your brain will have a harder time functioning their very best. Also, you'll be more likely to get hangry (that feeling when you are so hungry you feel mad). The more regular, healthy meals and snacks you have throughout the day, the better you'll feel, the longer you'll feel full, and the better food choices you'll make.

Eating Disorders

An **eating disorder** is when someone has unhealthy thoughts and behaviors about food and their body. It's not just about wanting to be healthy or eat well; it becomes a big worry and takes up a lot of thoughts and space in their mind. People with eating disorders might eat too little or too much, and it can make them feel really stressed or upset. These thoughts and behaviors can affect their health and well-being.

Imagine if someone's brain is sending them messages about their body or the food they eat and it is making them feel bad, like, "Even though you're hungry, you shouldn't eat," or "You shouldn't have breakfast because you're too heavy." It's like having an unhelpful loud voice in their head. Those types of messages can take up a lot of your time too. There are different types of eating disorders, and they affect how people think about and eat food. Not everyone who has unhealthy thoughts about food and eating has an eating disorder, but if you're concerned that you might, it's important to talk to a trusted adult about how you're feeling.

There are many side effects from having eating disorders, like feeling weak or dizzy, not being able to poop normally, or causing problems with growth. Eating disorders can even hurt a person's heart, bones, and other important body parts. Sometimes, when eating disorders are really severe, people have to go to the hospital to keep their bodies safe.

But here's the important part: there are special doctors and helpers who know a lot about food and feelings. Getting help from doctors and therapists can be important to change those thoughts and behaviors and help people feel better about themselves and their relationship with food. Doctors can work with kids to help them eat better and be healthy. It's really important to talk to grown-ups like your parents, a school counselor, or your pediatrician if you or someone you know is having problems with food so you or they can get the right help. Everyone deserves to feel happy and healthy!

* * * * *

Greta grabbed an apple from the bowl on the kitchen counter and gave her dad a hug.

"Sometimes, it's hard for me to separate what sounds good at the moment from what will make my body feel good all day," Greta said.

"Sweetie, you're not the only one," her dad said. "And learning how to fuel your body and pay attention to what it needs is something you'll do your entire life. It's something I'm still learning to do too. Let's keep learning together, okay?"

Greta nodded and gave her dad another hug.

CHAPTER 7

MOVING MY BODY

Natalia started using a wheelchair when they were 3 years old. But when they were old enough to understand, Natalia's parents let them know they had a condition called cerebral palsy.

Using a wheelchair meant using their body much differently than their friends used theirs. They couldn't run, jump, or hop. But they still moved *a lot.* In fact, Natalia's parents sometimes said their arms had superstrength from all that pushing around school they did. And Natalia even knew how to dance in their wheelchair. And they loved to dance and sing. Once, they hosted a sing-along birthday party, and all their friends took turns swinging around the dance floor with them to the music.

At Camp Corazón, Natalia didn't participate in every activity the camp had to offer, but all their friends seemed surprised by how many events they could do, thanks to the support of the administrators, their camp counselor, and their friends. They swam with supports, played tennis, and learned wheelchair yoga.

After camp ended, Natalia kept exploring new ways to move their body. Their best friend, Addie, took selfies of them in a local 4k walk/roll/run. They used their arm braces to propel them forward as fast as possible.

"We look so FIRE!" Natalia said. "I'm sending this to Juan right now."

* * * * *

Exercise

Moving your body is sooooooo good for you. Not only does it make your physical body strong and healthy, but it also helps your brain function the way it's supposed to and keeps your mental health on track. Here are some of the key reasons why exercise is important for our bodies.

Heart Health

Exercise strengthens the heart and improves blood circulation so your body can deliver nutrients and oxygen to your entire body effectively. It can improve overall heart health.

Fuel Efficiency

Staying active helps your body use all the fuel (carbohydrates, protein, and fats) you get from food most efficiently. That means it helps your body not waste the energy you give it or hold onto energy it doesn't need.

Muscle and Bone Health

Weight-bearing and resistance exercises, like swimming and rock climbing, help your muscles develop and grow stronger. Regular exercise makes your bones sturdy and healthy so they don't break easily.

Flexibility and Balance

Stretching and flexibility exercises like yoga or aerial dance help keep your joints in good shape and make it less likely you'll get injured. Activities that challenge balance, like gymnastics or bike riding, can help prevent falls and keep your core strong so you can play more easily.

Mental Health Benefits

Exercise helps you release chemicals in your body called *endorphins,* which are natural mood lifters.

Improved Sleep Quality

Regular body movement can help you have a more restful night's sleep.

Enhanced Cognitive Function

Exercise improves how fast and how well your brain works, including your memory and attention. That means paying attention in class and working on your homework (or your chores at home) may be a little easier!

Immune System Support

Regular exercise may help the body fight off infections like colds and the flu and reduce the risk of **chronic diseases** (diseases that affect you for a long time).

Less Stress

Physical activity can act as a natural stress reliever, helping you manage big emotions and anxiety. It provides an outlet for pent-up energy and helps the body and mind relax.

Social Interaction

Exercising with others can help you make and keep friends, learn teamwork, and have fun with other kids your age.

How Much Movement Your Body Needs

Your body's movement needs to change with your age. Once you reach elementary school age, doctors recommend you engage in at least 60 minutes of body movement every day. That doesn't mean you need to do it all at once, though! Daily movement adds up fast when you walk to school for 10 minutes, ride your bike for 20 minutes, dance to your favorite songs for 15 minutes, and stretch with your dad for 15 minutes before bed.

Most importantly, moving your body should be fun! Some kids like exercising with their friends in an organized sport like soccer, basketball, or baseball. Other kids have more fun on their own or in activities that don't require any equipment, like dancing in their living rooms to their favorite songs or doing movement activities that don't seem like exercise at all, like playing freeze tag or dodgeball, and that's totally okay! It's all about whatever activities bring you the most joy!

My Turn | Getting Enough Exercise

Keep track of how much you move and groove. Count all those steps, jumps, and dance moves.

For each day of the week, fill in how close you got to 60 minutes a day.

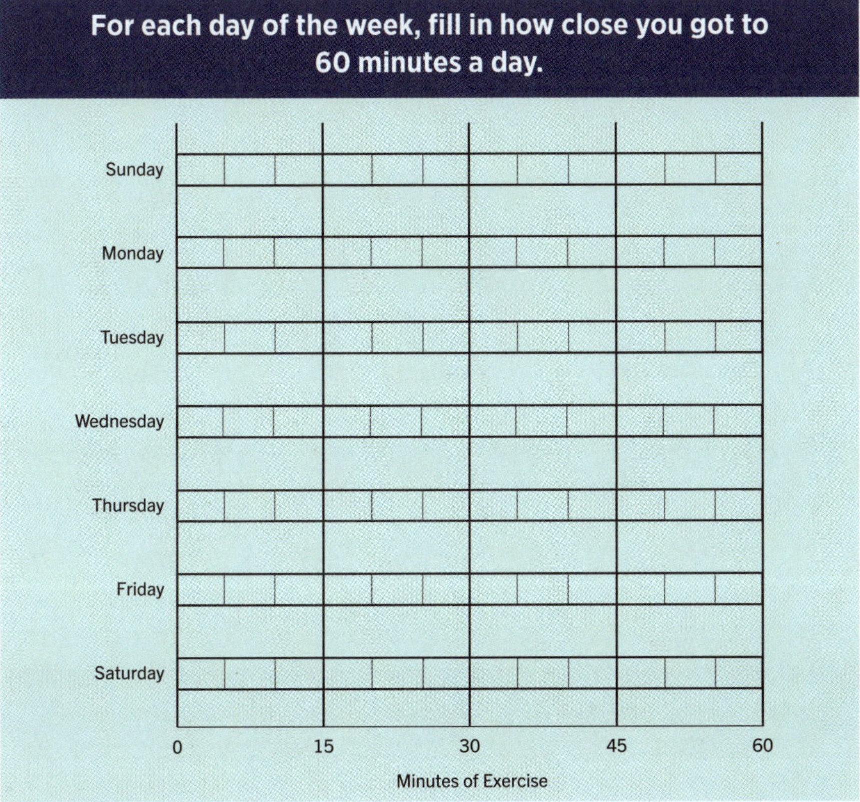

If you didn't get much exercise last week, that's important information, but it doesn't mean there's something wrong with you—it just means you haven't found the type of movement you love best yet! Let's look at different options for movement that fit your personality, fit your individual body needs, and feel like fun. Once you decide on a type of movement you want to try, talk to your parents about how to get involved.

Movement, Movement, So Many Types of Movement!

Everyone has different types of movement that fit best with their individual fitness levels, interests, and skills. And there are a lot of different types of movement out there that you may have never heard of or never tried. Who knows? If you try a new form of movement, you may just find something that's a perfect fit for you! Remember, too, when you try a new sport or type of movement, it's normal to feel a little awkward or unsure how you feel about it at first. Give it a little time if that's the case for you.

My Turn | My Kind of Movement

Think about all the movement activities you have tried before and liked.

Circle the activities listed below that you have tried before. Maybe you will be inspired to try them again!		
Soccer	Ultimate Frisbee	Figure skating
Basketball	Running	Martial arts (such as tae kwon do or karate)
Football	Swimming	
Rugby	Dance	Tennis
Cricket	Rock climbing	Gymnastics
Baseball	Canoeing	Yoga
Softball	Kayaking	Walking
Field hockey	Hiking	Aerial arts
Ice hockey	Parkour	Tag
Volleyball	Archery	Dodgeball
Handball	Surfing	Wrestling
Water polo	Diving	Other
Lacrosse	Skiing	

Now place a star next to the activities listed below you don't know much about but you are interested in trying them.		
Soccer	Ultimate Frisbee	Figure skating
Basketball	Running	Martial arts (such as tae kwon do or karate)
Football	Swimming	
Rugby	Dance	Tennis
Cricket	Rock climbing	Gymnastics
Baseball	Canoeing	Yoga
Softball	Kayaking	Walking
Field hockey	Hiking	Aerial arts
Ice hockey	Parkour	Tag
Volleyball	Archery	Dodgeball
Handball	Surfing	Wrestling
Water polo	Diving	Other
Lacrosse	Skiing	

Movement is for everybody, everywhere! It's important to remember that. Depending on our individual body types and health conditions, where we live, the way our brains are wired, or if we have a disability, we may need to adjust what types of exercises we do. If you live in a surfing city in California, you might not be skiing anytime soon this summer (unless you travel!). Even though Natalia needs to stay in their wheelchair or use their arm braces while moving their body, they can still exercise.

My Turn | My Unique Exercise Needs

Take a minute and think about the activities that you like to do.

Answer the questions below in the space provided.
How the place I live and what I have at home help me decide which exercises I can try:
How my body affects what types of exercises I can do:

A Growth Mindset Around Movement

Greta didn't feel like doing *anything*. Not reading. Not building with Lego bricks. Not baking. All she wanted to do was stare at her iPad, play Minecraft, and completely zone out. It was the second day of holiday break and she'd already lost all motivation. No school + no friends around = lazy days. Her dad had other plans, though.

"Hey kiddo," he said, bounding into the room. "Let's go do something fun together. We can take a walk, ride bikes, play *Just Dance* on TV. What'll it be?"

Greta rolled over in bed, even more annoyed and tired now that her space had been invaded.

"Ugh. I just want to be by myself today. I don't feel like doing anything. Why do I even have to move?"

Her dad sighed. "Honey, we've got to be active today. You can choose what kind of movement we do, but it's important that we do it."

* * * * *

It can be challenging to motivate ourselves to be active. Sometimes, it's not our bodies that keep us from moving; it's our minds. We become hesitant if we haven't tried a new type of exercise that we fear we won't be any good at, it will be hard to learn, or we'll embarrass ourselves when we first attempt it. Thinking about moving our bodies in a new way can make us feel nervous or unsure. Or maybe we just haven't moved in a while and thinking about getting off the couch sounds like SO. MUCH. WORK.

Here are a few strategies you can use if you feel anxious about trying a new type of exercise or if you haven't exercised in a while and are having a tough time getting going. These are part of a concept called **growth mindset,** which we'll talk about more in Chapter 9.

- **Start small.** Learn just one skill related to the sport or exercise at a time. Interested in basketball? Start by practicing your dribbling.
- **Find other newbies.** Ask your friends if anyone else is new to the activity like you are. Once you know who else wants to find out more about the new activity you want to try, you can learn together.
- **Practice, practice, practice.** Hardly anyone is good at skiing on their first attempt. If you fall the first time, keep on practicing until you're better—either with other new learners, on your own, or with someone who is already more skilled than you.
- **Don't be afraid of mistakes.** Most of the best athletes out there have had major flops at some time or another during their careers. A missed free throw at a championship basketball game or a botched jump at the ice-skating finals doesn't make those athletes failures; it makes them human. The athletes who consider mistakes as opportunities to get better, grow from them instead of being discouraged by them, are the ones who have staying power. Deciding that you're doing well at something by giving your best effort and learning, even if you're not perfect at it, is called having a growth mindset.

My Turn | Growth Mindset Strategies

From the list below, circle the growth mindset strategy you have tried in the past when participating in a new activity. Then make a star next to the mindset strategies you are willing to try in the future.

Don't be afraid of mistakes.	Find other newbies.
Practice, practice, practice.	Start small.

Working Your Body Too Hard

"Ouch! My leg!" Hayley fell to the floor in the gym, her foot searing in pain. She'd been working out nonstop for the past month to get ready for the state gymnastics competition, without more than a day off in the last 2 weeks. When she woke up this morning, she felt ready for anything, but during warm-ups, her legs were wobbly. *Maybe it's just nerves,* she thought to herself. Now, though, she wasn't so sure.

She was just finishing her floor routine. It ended with a front handspring into a front tuck and then into a middle split, something she'd practiced over and over again, but something just felt...off. When she landed, she heard the crunch right away, and then the pain came next. An hour later, she found herself in her pediatrician's office and heard her doctor say the words she feared most: "Hayley, you'll need to take some time off. You broke your foot."

When we work our bodies too hard, it can be really unsafe. Just like your body needs movement, it also needs rest. And, maybe most importantly, it needs you to listen to it. When you exercise, if you feel pain, have difficulty breathing, or feel like fainting, that means it's time to take a break.

If you feel tired or something doesn't feel right—like if your knee starts hurting after basketball practice or you get a headache after a game of tag—take a break and tell a grown-up.

Mottos like "No pain, no gain," "Push through the discomfort," or "Pain is temporary, gains are permanent," are unhealthy for your growing young body. The sports world is becoming more and more focused on health and safety for kids, but sometimes you'll still hear coaches (or even parents) say these mottos as they try to encourage you to do your best. In this case, it's best to listen to your body more than you listen to those well-intentioned adults. Your body is like your best friend—listen to what it's saying!

My Turn | Listening to My Body

Practice tuning into one part of your body for 30 seconds. Allow yourself to become quiet and to focus on the one area you want to notice. Breathe in and out gently so your mind can really pay attention to that one body part.

In the space provided, list the things you felt, saw, or heard.

Example: I heard my heart thumping. It sped up when I took a breath in. It slowed down when I breathed out. I felt the beating in my chest when I put my hand over my heart. I felt calm.

Here are some ways you can make sure your body has what it needs to move without injuries before you ever start exercising.

Get Ready to Move

Before you start playing or doing exercises, spend a few minutes doing easy movements to warm up your muscles. It's like telling your body, "Hey, get ready for some fun!"

Use the Right Moves

When you're playing sports or doing exercises, try to copy the right moves. If you're not sure, ask a grown-up or coach to show you.

Wear the Right Stuff

Put on comfy shoes and any protective gear you need, like a bike helmet when you ride your bike or elbow pads and kneepads for roller-skating. Make sure you ask an adult to help remind you when you need new equipment. Sometimes, exercising in worn-out shoes or shoes that are too tight can cause pain in your feet and legs.

Start Slow, Then Go

Don't rush into superhard exercises. Start easy and then add more challenges as you become stronger. It's like leveling up in a video game!

Have a Helper

If you're playing a sport or doing activities, have a grown-up or coach watch you.

Drink Water

Don't forget to drink water when you work out. It helps you stay hydrated and strong and ready for action!

Take Rest Stops

Every body needs rest. Take time off to rest and recharge, especially when you have an injury. Your doctor can help you decide how much time you need to take off if you get hurt.

Cooldown Time

After all the fun, do some easy stretches to help your muscles cool down.

Try Different Super Moves

Try different activities and sports. This will help you figure out what you like best and what you feel really good at (though you don't have to be good at an activity or sport to enjoy it!).

Follow the Rules

If you're playing a game, pay attention to all the rules your coach and teammates tell you to follow.

Turn Up the Team Spirit!

It's not about who wins or loses but how you play the game, the friends you make, and supporting one another to do your best. And having fun, of course!

My Turn | Keeping My Body Safe During Exercise

Answer the questions below in the space provided.
How I keep my body safe when I'm exercising:
Extra steps I learned and will now do to keep my body safe when I am exercising:

* * * * *

"Watch me do a wheelie!" Natalia laughed as they spun around and around with their cabinmates at the Camp Corazón dance party. "Love Story" blared through the gymnasium speakers as the campers sang along to Taylor Swift.

"Watch me do the worm," Juan challenged back, dropping to his belly and lifting up and down with his arms and legs. He moved awkwardly around the gym floor, the rest of his friends trying to follow his silly dance moves.

Even Greta joined in the fun.

"Hey, you're exercising!" Molly called to her from across the room.

"I am?" Greta called back.

"Yeah, and you're having fun doing it!"

"I am!" Greta grinned from ear to ear.

"We are!" said Natalia, high-fiving their friends.

CHAPTER 8

I AM WHAT I WATCH

Not watching screens for a whole week at Camp Corazón was tough for Juan. He was used to watching sports most days with his best friend, Jason, after school, and most weekends too. It took a couple days at camp for his body and brain to get used to not having constant input from a phone, tablet, or television. Slowly, though, Juan found that more time away from screens meant more time for noticing the real world around him: the sound of kids splashing in the pool, the smell of Mrs Johnson's biscuits, and the feeling of adrenaline pumping through his veins as he waited his turn for the ropes course.

For as long as he could remember, Juan wanted to play professional football. It was his dream to play in the big game, just like his favorite players. Every week during football season, he watched the games with his dad and sister, rooting loudly for Dallas and against San Francisco. Juan didn't just want to play football, though; he wanted to be just like the football players he watched on television week after week. They strode out onto the field each game, all cool, calm, and collected—ready for victory. Juan had posters of his favorite players taped to his walls and talked about the best plays of the week with his buddies at lunch most days. They also kept up on the latest fitness routines the top teams and players used to stay in tip-top shape. The players all looked mean and lean, ready to attack on the field.

"Man, I want abs and biceps like that," Jason told him as they walked home from school. Juan and Jason planned to review the new plays that their coach taught them at practice earlier that day. "My brother had abs during wrestling season in high school, but do you know what he had to do? He had to basically starve himself for a week to be able to compete in the wrestling weight class his coach assigned. It was so bad. He was tired and dizzy the whole time. My mom says that was waaaaay unhealthy. His doctor said he shouldn't do that again—it could make him really sick."

"Really?" asked Juan. "My cousin's team is very careful about stuff like that. The coach doesn't make anyone cut weight when it's not healthy. They even make the kids do something called a water test to make sure no one is dehydrated before they compete."

Jason and Juan had been playing football, soccer, and baseball together for as long as they could remember. Jason was always up for a pickup game, but he was also someone good to talk to when you felt like you needed a friend.

Juan stared down at his own skinny arms and stomach. Somehow, even though they didn't know him and never would, he thought of the guys on Dallas as teammates. He felt like he didn't measure up to them at all and that he never would, even as he got older—no matter how hard he tried. He had a feeling, but he couldn't quite put his finger on what it was; all he knew was that he really didn't like the body he was in, and he wished he was living in theirs.

* * * * *

Technology is amazing! Just think of all the exciting things you learned just this week on your tablet, computer, television, or smartphone. Want to learn to speak Italian? No problem. Ready to explore the history of Japanese shrines and traditions? It's at your fingertips. Interested in newly discovered ocean life or Greek mythology? Coming right up! From exotic recipes to technological advancements, we can access anything and everything from the comfort of our homes—anytime we want.

But just because we can see and hear it all, all the time, on the internet doesn't mean we should. I know as you read this you might be rolling your eyes, but finding a balance with screens is very important for your mental and physical health. For one thing, too much screen time (yes, even if it's time spent viewing good content) is bad for our brains. Pediatricians want kids to not use screens for more than 2 hours a day (that doesn't include times they need to use a screen for homework or at school), to keep screens out of their bedrooms, and to put their screens away anytime they're eating meals. They also recommend not using devices right before bedtime so kids can fall asleep more easily and sleep well through the night.

Screen Time Safety

Sometimes, when you are scrolling on a device, you might come across a site that is not appropriate for your viewing. Most websites and social media apps don't check to see how old you are when you access them. What they talk about or show may be meant for adults, not kids or teens. They may use adult words, talk about adult subjects, or show adult images that aren't meant for you. That means some of the content you consume may be inappropriate for you. At some point, you will come across something that your eyes, ears, heart, or mind is not quite ready for. When that happens, it's important to tell a trusted adult.

My Turn | How I'm Doing Staying Safe While I Use Screens

For each topic below, circle the face that matches best.	
Not Using Screens Too Much	😀 🙂 😐 🙁 ☹️
Avoiding Content I Don't Want to Mimic	😀 🙂 😐 🙁 ☹️
Putting Away My Screen When I'm Told To	😀 🙂 😐 🙁 ☹️

Parental Controls

Here's some good news, though! You don't have to practice internet safety alone. Your parents can set what are called **parental controls** on your devices to make sure you can enjoy the internet without worry. Parental controls are limits on what's available to you based on your age or based on what your parents think is okay for you. They're designed to keep you safe without you having to decide what's okay and what's not (I know, I know, you don't want your parents controlling every little move you make, but it's important they keep tabs on what you see and hear as you explore your digital world). That way, you don't accidentally stumble on information or images that aren't appropriate for you.

Parental controls are not your responsibility, but it is important that you know about them so you can understand why you might not be able to access certain apps or websites on your devices. These controls can be regulations on how much time you spend on devices, what internet sites you visit, or what types of content you view on any website.

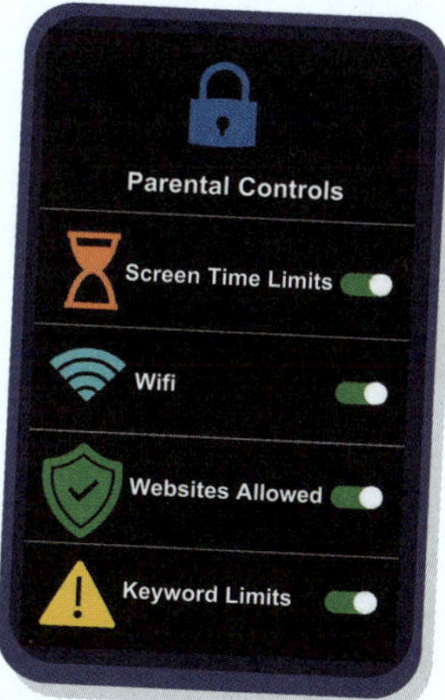

My Turn | Parental Controls

Make sure to talk to your family about the parental controls in your house and why they exist.

Answer the question below in the space provided.

These are the parental controls we have to help keep me safe.

Fake Images = Real Bad Feelings About Ourselves

Juan was reading up on the score of last night's professional soccer game and noticed how his favorite player looked perfect at the press conference after playing for almost 2 hours. He flashed a smile at the cameras and talked easily with the journalists. Juan immediately felt bad about what he looked like after playing soccer during lunch at school. Why couldn't he be perfect too?

* * * * *

What you see and hear on the internet affects the way you think about yourself. For example, when kids only see images of people who have perfectly clear skin (or who use social media filters to make their skin look perfectly clear), it makes them think everyone needs to have perfect skin. You and I may know that it's normal to have a few blemishes or dry patches (or a lot of them!) as we grow up, but when we see all those pictures of fake, blemish-free, silky-smooth complexions, it can make us forget what's real. And, what's worse, it can make us feel terrible about the blemished, imperfect skin we have (and potentially make us spend a lot of time and money trying to make our skin look like what we see on a screen). Not only do the platforms filter and alter images, but they also create algorithms so that kids see more and more content that is similar to what they're looking for. Which means, if a person is looking at social media on topics around thin bodies or running or faces or hips or thighs, the algorithm will pick up on that and they will see more and more images or videos like that.

The same things happen in our brain when we spend too much time on the internet seeing unrealistic body images, especially on social media, but we don't even realize it most of the time. When it comes to accepting and loving the bodies we're in, some of the most harmful images we see on social media are photos of influencers who enhance how they look with technology. Almost every platform lets people use filters or computer programs to make themselves look like they have clearer skin, thinner thighs, or fuller lips. And the more kids like you see those images, the more you forget that they're total fakes!

In the same way, when we spend a lot of time playing unrealistic video games that show situations or people that aren't real life, our brains can get confused about what's reality and what's unrealistic. The real reality is, everybody is different, and you are amazing just the way you are. When you stop comparing yourself to other people, you can start believing in you!

Seeing too many celebrity images in our social media feeds can also trick our brains into thinking everyone's body should look like a famous athlete, a movie star, or a pop star. The reality is that a lot of famous performers and athletes spend hours and hours a day exercising or don't eat in a way that gives their bodies the right kind of energy to look the way they do. They spend most of their time focused on maintaining or improving their appearance. Many also go to specialty doctors to have operations that change how their noses, teeth, cheeks, lips, hips, or tummies look. Others just have different body types than we do.

Other than helping Juan perfect his blocking and passing skills, what else does staring at pictures of famous football players whose bodies aren't like his help Juan do? Not much. Even though Juan is mostly reading about players to learn more about their stats, he's also spending a lot of time wishing his body type was a lot more like theirs than his own. He'd give anything to be the ripped star quarterback or running back of a winning team, but his body may not be built for those positions. His thinner body type may be more suited for a spot as a receiver. Bigger bodies tend to fill offensive or defensive line spots.

The same thing happens when he watches online videos of all those "perfect" bodies that aren't like his. They make him feel even less perfect about his own body—and make him want to change his body to be something it's naturally not. A research study even found that the more teens use social media, the more depression symptoms they have, *and* the more they see images that have been changed to look more "perfect," the more they can have feelings of low self-esteem and body dissatisfaction.

Genes + Environment

Everyone in Juan's family was thin—his sister, Carissa; his mom, Maria; his dad, Jose; and Juan. No matter how much sour cream he added to his mom's enchiladas or how many taquitos he ate, he still looked in the mirror and saw someone who looked thin but not muscular. Building strong muscles is important for kids of all sizes and shapes. Juan thought about spending extra time in the garage lifting weights and trying to gain weight, but he knew it could leave him sore and maybe even injured if he lifted too much or incorrectly tried to be just like his favorite players. To understand how to build strength for his body type, Juan needed to understand 2 major factors that make our bodies look the way they do: **genes** and **environment**.

Genes are the building blocks of our bodies. They're made up of DNA passed down from our parents and they "wire" us a certain way—a way we

can't change, even if we want to. Juan, for example, has black hair and brown eyes. That's because both of those traits are in his family genes. And even if he closes his eyes really tight and wishes for his hair to be pink and his eyes to be silver, they won't be. Genes also decide what size and shape your body will be. Just like your nose may look like your great-aunt Edna's, your hips may look like your uncle Ned's. Genes influence how tall we are, how much we weigh, and how much muscle we have.

Environment is everything in and around our bodies. It's the place we live, how many sidewalks we have for walking or bike paths we have for riding. It's the food we have available to eat, the way that food is prepared, and how often your grandma tells you to have another serving as she pinches your cheeks. It's the culture we grow up in—the tamales our family makes every Christmas or the special biryani our aunt serves at family gatherings. It's the way we move our bodies, the amount of time we spend on our devices, and the amount of sleep we get. And even though genes are *really* important when it comes to who we are and how we look, environment matters just as much.

Body-Negative Content

When you view online ads or TV commercials that focus on tricks and tips for getting or staying a certain size by not eating enough or by exercising too much, that is also inappropriate for kids and teens. When you see too much of this body-negative content, it can make your brain think about it over and over. Instead of focusing on choosing foods based on how they'll help your body function, it can make you focus on how they'll make your body look. Instead of thinking about how movement will help your body keep working well, it can make you think about how different exercises will make your body appear.

It's normal as human beings (and especially preteens and teens!) to care about our appearance, but how we look is not all that matters about us. Sadly, though, seeing unrealistic and weight-focused content on social media or online can make us think that we're only valuable if we look a certain way. It can flood our brains with false ideas about what kind of bodies are good and how good we are (or aren't!) if our bodies don't match what we see. That's why it's so important that we pay attention to what we consume on the internet and why we have to make healthy decisions for ourselves about what we'll watch.

My Turn | How Healthy Is My Media Use?

Write down a few of your favorite shows, movies, social media channels, or games you watch or play in the space provided below.

With those shows, movies, and games in mind, answer each question below, placing a check mark in the column that best fits.				
	✓ Never	✓ Sometimes	✓ Often	✓ Not Sure
How often do they encourage me to have healthy habits?				
How often do they show people from different cultures or backgrounds?				
How often do they show inappropriate content (violence, bad words, suggestive content, bullying)?				
How often do they show content that's fake (filters/changed using technologically)?				
How often do they show content that's unrealistic (celebrities or influencers)?				
How often do they show content that's based on stereotypes?				
How often do they show content that makes me feel bad about my body?				
How often do they show content to try to get me to buy something I don't actually need?				

Your Body, Your Mind, Your Internet Content

Here's the great news! Lots of people who put information on the internet want to make sure you have positive role models and plenty of content that's healthy for you. Look for content that focuses on

- Including a lot of different types of people as actors (different skin types, different perspectives, and different genders)
- Demonstrating kindness, community, problem-solving, and a growth mindset
- Showing real bodies, not altered or unrealistic ones
- Highlighting a healthy relationship with food and exercise

My Turn | My Screen Time Choices

Work with your parents to find some healthy screen options for you. For example, family games, relaxation apps, educational apps, physical activity apps, language learning apps, or music learning apps can all be fun and good for you!

In the space below, write down 4 or 5 healthy screen options you and your parents came up with.
1.
2.
3.
4.
5.

Screen Time Alternatives

Even though watching screens can be fun, it's important to spend your time doing other activities you love too! When we spend too much time on screens—or when we make screens our go-to activity when we're bored—we miss out on tons of other even more amazing experiences. Also, when we use devices as our go-to way of dealing with boredom (or to fill the time when there's nothing else to do), our brains don't learn how to be okay just *being,* doing nothing at all. And knowing how to do nothing at all is super important for us. It gives us time to learn what our surroundings are like, how to communicate with others, and how to navigate social situations.

Because using screens all the time is easy for adults and kids to do, it can be helpful to write down activities you enjoy that *aren't* related to screens ahead of time so that, the next time you're bored, you can look back at the list and remind yourself of all the screen time alternatives you have.

My Turn | Screen-Free Activities I Love

Listed below are some examples of screen-free activities.

Reading	Baking	Exercise
Going for a walk	Gardening	Playing with my pets
Playing card games	Writing	Drawing
Making craft projects	Talking with friends	Painting

Write down the top 10 screen-free activities you want to try next time you're bored.

1.

2.

3.

4.

5.
6.
7.
8
9.
10.

* * * * *

A tiny little bird landed on the cabin porch just as Juan stepped outside and sat on the steps. It had been 6 days since he last went online. He'd found himself wishing he could watch football highlight reels over and over on Sunday and Monday, but it hadn't even crossed his mind all day today.

Usually, he had his head down when he walked, and his dad had to keep reminding him to look up and see the world around him, but not this week. This week he noticed little things, like the tiny bird who, now he saw, had made a small nest in the cabin's eaves.

"Tweet tweet," the bird sang to 5 little pink heads poking up and down in the nest, waiting for their mama to feed them.

"Tweet tweet," they answered back.

Juan smiled.

"Tweet tweet," he said, lacing up his shoes. He walked, head up so he wouldn't miss anything else amazing, toward his next in-the-moment camp adventure.

CHAPTER 9

MY MENTAL HEALTH MATTERS

D-E-S-P-I-C-A-B-L-E. Or was it D-I-S-P-I-C-A-B-L-E? "Come on, Hayley! Don't be so stupid. You should know this."

There were only 5 minutes left until the bell rang during English Language Arts, which meant only a few moments more to spell the last 10 words on her spelling test. The more the seconds clicked on, the more Hayley felt like a total loser—and the harder she got on herself.

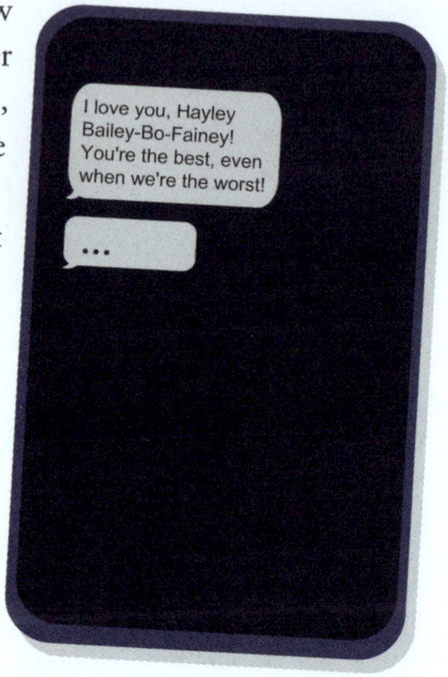

"I should have studied more. I shouldn't have watched that movie this weekend. I shouldn't have wasted all my time sleeping!" It was like a bully was taking over her mind, pushing her against a wall, stealing all her lunch money.

"Ugh, I give up! Why even try?"

When she got home, Hayley's mom was waiting at the door.

"Hi, honey! How was your day?" she asked.

"Terrible!" Hayley cried. "I think I failed my spelling test. I'm so disappointed in myself."

"Oh no. I'm sure you tried your best. Try not to be hard on yourself. While you were out, one of your camp friends sent you a message. Maybe it will cheer you up?"

Hayley brightened and looked down at the phone screen. There was a picture of she and Greta coming in last at the field day race, their arms held high holding a "Best Try" trophy as they cheered.

* * * * *

Just like all bodies are different, so are all minds. The way your mind works is based on your family history, your experiences, and your environment (the people you're surrounded by, the place you live, and the school you go to). They influence your **personality** (the characteristics, qualities, and/or traits that form your character) and your **temperament** (the way you behave naturally or respond to the world around you—for example, some people are really calm, while others are super energetic or sensitive). Most of these factors are things you have absolutely no control over. They won't change anytime soon, even if you want them to!

Your **mental health** is your overall well-being when it comes to how you think and feel. Because every person on the planet has a mind, we all have mental health (just like because every person has a body, we all have physical health). One thing to remember—mental health and mental illness are not the same thing. **Mental illness** is a medical condition that affects a person's thoughts, mood, or behavior. Mental illness can make it difficult for people to live their lives.

The wonderful news? There are tons of ways you can strengthen your mental health, no matter who you are.

Growth Mindset

Having a growth mindset is like having a special power in your brain. It means thinking about challenges and mistakes as opportunities to learn and become even better at something. The opposite of having a growth mindset is having a **fixed mindset.** A fixed mindset means thinking that you have a set amount of intelligence or talent and there's not much you can do to change it. It's a bit like believing you're stuck with the skills you have and can't really become better.

Let's say you're trying to solve a tricky math problem. If you have a growth mindset, you may think, "I might not get it right away, but that's okay! Mistakes help me learn, and with practice, I can figure it out." It's like imagining your brain is like a muscle that gets stronger when you use it. The more you practice, try new things, and learn from mistakes, the smarter and more skilled you become. So, having a growth mindset is believing you can improve and get better at anything if you keep trying and learning.

If you have a fixed mindset, you might think, "I'm not good at math problems. I'll never be good at them." Instead of seeing math problems as a challenge to learn from, you might feel like giving up because you don't believe you can get better. Just like Hayley wanted to give up on her spelling exercise, someone with a fixed mindset might say, "I'm not good at this, and I'll never be good at it, so why bother trying?" But the thing is, our brain is like a muscle, and with practice and effort, we can get better at anything! So, having a fixed mindset can sometimes make it harder to learn and grow because you're not open to the idea that you can improve with time and effort.

Resilience

Resilience is like being a bouncy rubber ball. Sometimes in life, things might not go the way you want them to. It could be something difficult or sad, like not doing well on a test or facing a problem with friends. When you are resilient, you can bounce back from those tough situations, even if it takes a lot of hard work. Just like a rubber ball can bounce back after being thrown on the ground, being resilient helps you come back strong after facing challenges. It's all about being strong on the inside and finding ways to keep going, no matter what happens. Resilience is also about building relationships. The more you surround yourself with a strong, connected culture, family, and group of friends, the more they'll help you to bounce back too.

The 7 Cs of Resilience

Dr Kenneth Ginsburg, a pediatrician and an expert in resilience, breaks it into what he calls the 7 Cs.

Competence

What is competence? Being really good at dealing with different situations and getting better by doing things and learning from them.

Why does it matter? It helps you trust your own choices, make smart decisions, and handle tough situations.

Example: Learning how to ride a bike. At first, it might be tricky, but with practice and experience, you become competent, and soon you can ride confidently.

Confidence

What is confidence? Really believing in yourself and what you can do.

Why does it matter? It helps you face challenges in life with a positive attitude.

Example: Giving a presentation in class. If you believe in yourself and your abilities, you'll stand tall, speak clearly, and feel good about sharing your ideas.

Connection

What is connection? Having strong relationships with family, friends, school, and your community.

Why does it matter? It keeps you from doing things just to get attention in a bad way.

Example: Spending time with family and friends. Sharing moments, talking, and being there for each other creates strong connections that make you feel supported and loved.

Character

What is character? Knowing what's right and wrong and sticking to your values and caring for others.

Why does it matter? It makes you feel good about yourself and helps you be confident.

Example: Helping a friend who is being bullied. Even if it's tough, sticking up for what's right and being kind shows good character and loving and supporting others.

Contribution

What is contribution? Understanding that you can make the world a better place as an individual.

Why does it matter? It gives you a purpose and makes you want to do things that make the world better.

Example: Volunteering to clean up a local park. By taking actions to better the environment, you contribute to the well-being of your community and the world.

Coping

What is coping? Being able to handle and deal with challenges in life using different strategies.

Why does it matter? If you know how to handle stress, you can overcome tough situations better.

Example: Having a bad day and talking to a friend about it or drawing to express your feelings. These are coping strategies that help you handle challenging situations.

Control

What is control? Knowing that you can influence what happens based on your decisions.

Why does it matter? If you think you have control over your choices, you'll be more active and positive. If you think what happens to you in life is completely up to everything that happens around you, you might feel like there's not much you can do to make your life better.

Example: Choosing to brush your teeth. When you take control of your dental hygiene, you have a better chance of not having cavities.

My Turn | The 7 Cs

Imagine you had an awful day at school, and then your friend had to cancel your laser tag game plans. Now your mom says you have to watch your little sister while she has a meeting for work. Worse day ever!

In the space below write down what you can do to help deal with all your big, negative feelings.

Which of the 7 Cs below can you use to help you?
Competence:
Confidence:
Connection:
Character:
Contribution:
Coping:
Control:

Mindfulness

Mindfulness is training your mind to be aware and focused on the present moment. It's about paying attention to what's happening right now without getting caught up in worries about the past or the future. Another way to think about it is keeping your mind where your body is.

Imagine your mind is a camera. When you're mindful, it's like zooming in on the current scene and really noticing the details. For example, if you're eating a slice of pizza, being mindful means you savor each bite, feel the textures, and enjoy the taste without thinking about other things.

Mindfulness also involves being aware of your thoughts and feelings without judging them or yourself for feeling these emotions. It's like watching clouds passing by in the sky—you observe them without saying they're good or bad. This helps you understand yourself better and deal with challenges more calmly.

Practicing mindfulness can involve simple activities, like taking deep breaths, focusing on your senses, or doing a body scan to check in with how you feel. It's like a superpower for your mind that helps you stay calm and focused and appreciate the present moment.

My Turn | Practice Mindfulness

Set a timer for 2 minutes. Sit with your eyes open and notice your breath going in and out of your body. Notice one thing that you hear, that you smell, and that you see. Now close your eyes. Focus on your breath. As little thoughts fill in and out of your mind, just notice them. Stay in this one place, with your eyes closed, until your timer goes off.

Try this mindfulness exercise for 2 minutes and answer the questions below. Tomorrow try it for 3 minutes and see how many minutes you can build up to this week.
What did you hear?
What did you smell?
What did you see?

Talk Kindly to Yourself (and Others)

Being Kind to Ourselves

Did you know that we all spend a lot of time every day thinking and talking to ourselves? How we talk to ourselves can make a huge difference in the way we see ourselves, the way we feel, and the way we treat other people. That's why paying attention to the way we think—and having tools in our toolbox for when our thinking is unkind or unfair to ourselves—is so important.

One of the best ways to be kind to ourselves is to practice talking to ourselves the way a best friend would treat us when we're feeling down or negative (which *will* happen from time to time because we're all human!). A good friend comforts us when we're sad, encourages us when we're hard on ourselves, and listens without judgment, especially if we're feeling scared, sad, or mad. We can act just like a best friend to ourselves using a technique called **mindful self-compassion:** treating ourselves with kindness and compassion in the moment. Here's how mindful self-compassion works.

Step 1: Name the Feelings

Notice and name whatever feeling or emotion you're having. Maybe you're feeling sad, lonely, or disappointed. If you can't tell *what* feeling you're having, notice what is happening in your body. For example, "My heart is beating fast," "My eyes are about to water," or "My chest feels tight," are all great clues as to what you're feeling. Even more basic? Paying attention to when you feel comfortable versus uncomfortable is a great start. A trusted adult (like a school counselor, a parent, or a grandparent) can help you use these descriptions of what's happening in your body to label the feelings they're attached to.

Step 2: Validate the Feelings

That means telling yourself it makes sense you have that feeling based on the circumstances you're in. For example, "It makes sense I feel lonely. I just moved to a new school and don't have many friends yet."

Step 3: Remember You're Not the Only One

That means reminding yourself that there are lots of other people who would feel exactly the same way you do if they were in your shoes. For example, "I bet there are tons of new kids at other schools right now who also feel lonely. I'm not alone."

My Turn | Practice Mindful Self-Compassion

Think about a time in the last week you weren't kind to yourself.

Write down how you could have practiced more mindful self-compassion.
Step 1: Name the feeling. Explain how you were feeling.
Step 2: Validate the feeling. How could you validate it?
Step 3: Remember you're not the only one. How could you remember it's not just you?

Talking Kindly to Others

"Dad, Elise told me I have a 'jelly belly.' Was that okay for her to say?" Greta was sprawled out on the floor of her bedroom, Lego pieces scattered all around her. She'd been working on this particular project for the last 2 days and was just about done. She bit her lower lip as she concentrated on the colors in front of her.

Greta's dad needed a little more information before he could offer any advice. "Do you know why she said that?"

"Well, we were playing at recess, and we were making rhymes for different parts of our body. Like, Elise said she has 'bear hair' because her hair is brown, and Kira said she has 'moon pie eyes' because her eyes are blue and shiny like a full moon. They called Etta 'brace face' and Drew was 'bedhead.' Then they added 'jelly belly' to the list for me. I was laughing, but I wasn't sure if it was okay that I thought it was funny—or that they did."

"How did it make *you* feel when they used the word 'jelly' to describe your belly?" her dad asked. Greta looked up from her Lego pile, surprised by the question.

"Oh, I love my belly. It's jiggly. It's curvy. It looks like yours!" she exclaimed.

Greta's dad gave her an eyebrow raise.

"What matters most is that *you* set the rules for what's okay for other people to say about your body, honey," said Dad. "You always get to decide, and it's always okay for you to speak up if someone says something you don't feel comfortable with. What you decide now might change depending on the day or even just as you get older. It's okay if it does."

Greta cocked her head to the side, feeling a bit confused. Sometimes, as part of having autism, it didn't make sense when the rules weren't set in stone. She asked her dad how she would know when it was right and when it was wrong. Greta's dad wrapped her into a tight hug.

"All kids have different words they feel comfortable with when it comes to their bodies," he explained. "Words like 'jelly belly,' 'brace face,' 'bedhead,' 'moon pie eyes'—even words like 'fat' that might seem negative to some people might be words that others use with pride. A lot of these words only seem negative to us because they have been used negatively for such a long time. It's important to never assume what words people feel comfortable with and to speak to other people with the intention of being kind."

* * * * *

My Turn | What Words Are Okay With Me?

Take a minute to think about what words are okay and what words are not okay for you when it comes to your body.

Answer the questions below in the space provided.
Words I don't want other people to use to describe my body:
Words I'm okay with other people using to describe my body:
If you're feeling brave, ask your friends what words they feel comfortable with when it comes to their own bodies and write them down here.

Handling Worries About Your Changing Body With Care

As your body changes through puberty, there may be times your friends grow faster or slower than you, that your skin erupts in pimples when it seems no one else's does, or that you feel unsure about one part of your body or another. That can make us feel incredibly self-conscious and can make it more challenging to love ourselves.

First, remember, it's normal to have worries as your body changes. This is all new, and it can all be scary! Second, remember, other kids also feel uncomfortable as their bodies change, even if they don't talk about it. You may start to see other kids and teens around you cover up skin blemishes with makeup or wear clothes to hide their bodies when they feel unsure of themselves. Then, remind yourself of how unique and amazing your body is. Go back to practicing kind words in the mirror, just like we did in the activity in Chapter 3, and to the basics of taking care of your body: moving it often, nourishing it well, allowing time for rest and relaxation, and focusing on hygiene, hydration, and caring for your mental health. You only have one body. It's sometimes awkward, but it's also unique and awesome! Your job is to take care of it—to love it! If you're still having trouble, talk to a trusted adult about how you're feeling so they can help.

My Turn | My Worries and Questions

Write down any worries or questions you have about your changing body, even if it feels silly to do it.

Write down the names of trusted adults you can talk to or ask questions about your changing body (a teacher, a parent, or someone else).

* * * * *

Hayley looked at her mom. "Well, that was perfect timing. You're right. I'm not going to give up. Do you think you could help me with studying tonight so I can retake the test tomorrow? They said we had a couple of chances."

"Of course I can," her mom responded. "But first, let's take a few minutes to rest and regroup. It might make it easier for you to focus, and it will definitely help you feel less anxious about tomorrow. How about we take a walk around the block?"

Hayley gave her mom a smile. "That sounds like just what I need."

CHAPTER 10

HOW TO LOVE MY BODY

"Until we meet again...."

As the song finished and the final fire sparks popped, all 5 campers could hardly believe their week at Camp Corazón had come to an end.

They'd learned so much about themselves and each other as they played, explored, and challenged themselves with new experiences and by making all kinds of new friends—and even though they didn't know it then, there would be even more to learn over the coming year.

Hayley, Greta, Natalia, Juan, and Troy were all completely different kids but, over the next 12 months, they would all struggle in some way or another with loving their bodies and with taking care of them. Good thing they had each other to lean on and that they'd learned lessons at Camp Corazón about body love that would last them not just a year, but a lifetime.

"...Happy trails to you, until we meet again. Happy trails to you, keep smiling until then."

The 5 campers gave one final smile and raised their wrists one more time to the sky.

"One more time!" Troy called out. "T-R-U-E-F-R-E-I-N-D-S forever!"

"Forever and always!" they all called back.

* * * * *

We receive so many messages every day about our bodies—from the images we see on screens, from our parents, from our friends, from our communities, and even from our own minds. Sometimes these messages are confusing. Sometimes they're hurtful. Sometimes they're unintentional. Remember, though, you don't have to listen to every message you hear.

When you think about the messages you hear, try to think of yourself as a screen, not a sponge. A sponge absorbs everything that comes its way. But we don't want to absorb everything that everyone says about us or what we say or think about ourselves. A screen, though, lets some things in and keeps some things out. When we are a screen, we can decide which messages we let in and which messages need to be kept out; just like a screen on a window, we will let in fresh air and sunshine but keep out bugs and rain.

Here's one empowering message you can hold onto day after day, no matter what else you hear: being body confident means taking care of it. And that means making sure it gets enough movement, rest, maintenance, hydration, nutrient-rich foods, and kindness. Your body is the only one you've got—and it deserves to be loved and cared for your whole life.

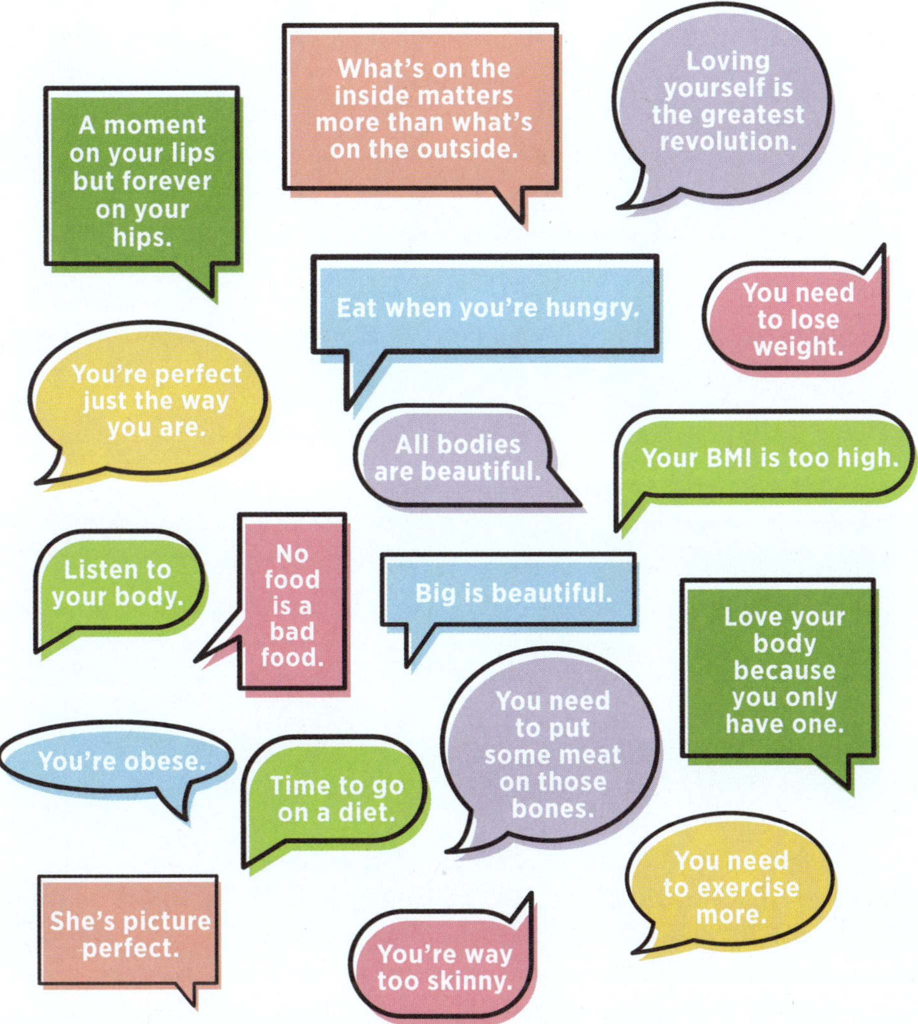

CHAPTER 11

MY BODY MATTERS

As you know, I am a pediatrician. As a doctor, it's my job to see young patients your age and make sure their bodies are healthy and growing strong. I do lots of things for my young patients your age. I see them at routine checkups where I check their vision and hearing; make sure their speech, muscle, and bone development is on track; and give vaccines to keep them safe from diseases that can be prevented. When kiddos are sick, I prescribe medicine to make them healthy. I ask lots of questions to make sure they are getting enough sleep, eating nutrient-rich food, and growing strong. I also remind kids to wear their bike helmets, apply sunscreen, and brush their teeth. It may not seem like it, but all those parts of my job are about helping you take care of your body. The thing is, I can't do it alone. Your body belongs to you. You're the most important part of your body's care team.

Now you know how important it is to take care of your one and only body, but, as your body grows and changes, you might have some questions about exactly how to do it. Remember, you can ask your pediatrician any questions that are on your mind! I promise you won't be the first kid to tell me how they feel about their body or to ask me questions about it. I see lots and lots of kids your age, and I want to share with you the questions I get asked, the things kids say every single day. My goal is to help you feel less alone if you feel like you're the only one who has ever had these kinds of thoughts or worries—and to give you some body tips to help yourself or a friend.

General Body Confidence

What Kids Say

"I don't feel good about any part of myself."

What I Say Back

"Your body is just one part of what makes you amazing. It doesn't define your heart, your mind, or your spirit—-and those are your real superpowers."

Body Tips

- It's okay to have changing feelings about your body as you grow.
- Your body will change a lot over time, especially during puberty, and it's normal to feel a mix of emotions about that.
- Sometimes you might feel awkward, excited, worried, or even confused about changes in your body. Many kids your age have mixed feelings about those changes.
- Loving your body doesn't mean you have to like everything about it all the time; it means learning to treat it with kindness.

Weight and Body Size

What Kids Say

"I wish I were skinnier like one of my friends."

What I Say Back

"Bodies come in all shapes and sizes, and one is not better than another. Your body is amazing because it helps you play, think, love, and grow—not because of how it looks. Don't compare yourself to others. Your body is special because it's yours. Talk to your parents before going to your next doctor's appointment. Share that you're feeling uncomfortable about your weight and ask them to start that conversation with your pediatrician. Remember, your goal is taking care of that one-of-a-kind body and your pediatrician is on your team to help you."

What Kids Say

"Today at school someone called me fat, and it made me really sad and embarrassed."

What I Say Back

"People sometimes say hurtful things when they don't understand that weight is not a measure of worth. Your body is not a problem to fix—it's a part of who you are, and it deserves respect. I am sorry they said that to you. Taking care of your body is important, and if you want to make changes, let's talk about it."

What Kids Say

"Why do all my friends talk about losing weight?"

What I Say Back

"Some people think being smaller means being healthier or more lovable, but that's just not true. Our health is about how we take care of our bodies, not how much we weigh. Let's check your weight on the scale to see where you are at."

Body Tips

- Taking care of your body makes it stay strong.
- Fueling your body with nutrient-rich foods, drinking water, and getting enough sleep helps it do incredible things like growing, healing, and thinking clearly.
- Superfoods like fruits, vegetables, proteins, and whole grains give your body the vitamins and nutrients it needs to stay powerful!
- Movement—whether it's dancing, playing sports, walking, or stretching—keeps your muscles and brain happy and healthy.

What Kids Say

"I think I need to eat less so I don't get fat, but I get hungry."

What I Say Back

"Food isn't something you have to avoid. Food gives us energy and helps us grow. Instead of worrying about being 'skinny,' let's think about how we can care for our bodies in a kind, respectful way. Eating all sweets isn't something anybody should do. We need to make sure we eat a balance of fruits, vegetables, and proteins each day. Let's take a look at what you are eating for each one of your meals together."

What Kids Say

"Why don't I look like the people I see on TV and in the movies?"

What I Say Back

"Most pictures on the internet are edited or posed. They aren't real life. Your body is real—and real bodies are strong, soft, wiggly, and wonderful. Your body is one of a kind—no one else in the world has the exact same body as you. That's something to be proud of. All bodies grow and change in different ways and at different times—and that's totally normal. Even things like height, weight, hair, and how we move or think can be different. That's what makes our world more interesting and beautiful."

Hair Differences

What Kids Say

"I hate my hair! It's too frizzy/curly/straight/weird/different."

What I Say Back

"Your hair has its own kind of magic. It doesn't need to look like anyone else's to be beautiful. I hear my patients say they want straight hair, thick hair, curly hair, another color than what they have. You can always try a fun new way to style your hair, if that helps you love it more. Talk to your parents about going to the salon or barber for help."

What Kids Say

"Why can't my hair be easier to take care of like everyone else's?"

What I Say Back

"I get that—it takes effort, and that can feel unfair. But your hair is part of what makes you YOU. Let's learn together how to take care of it in a way that feels good."

Acne and Skin Issues

What Kids Say

"My face looks gross with all this acne. What can I do to make it better?"

What I Say Back

"Acne is super common, especially during puberty, because that's a time when your hormones are changing—something you don't have any control over! Some people have more acne because of their skin type or because of what stage of puberty they're in. It doesn't make you dirty, ugly, or less lovable. It just means your body is doing exactly what it's supposed to. Taking care of your skin by cleansing it, moisturizing it, and protecting it from the sun will help it be the healthiest possible."

What Kids Say

"Sometimes I get really embarrassed by how my skin looks. What can I do to make it better?"

What I Say Back

"You're not alone—lots of people feel embarrassed about their skin. But no bump, rash, or pimple can change your worth or who you are inside. You're still you, and that's what people care about most. Even though it's tempting to buy lots of skin products meant for adults to 'fix' your skin, ask your parents and your pediatrician first. They'll make sure what you put on your skin is appropriate for you—and won't hurt your skin in the long run."

What Kids Say

"Why doesn't my skin look smooth like everyone else's?"

What I Say Back

"Nobody's skin is perfect. Not even the people in ads or on TV. Skin has pores, bumps, stretch marks, and scars—it's normal, even if it doesn't always seem that way from the images we see. Let's try to be kind to it, even on the tough days."

What Kids Say

"Why is my skin darker/lighter/more freckled/more bumpy than everyone else's?"

What I Say Back

"Our skin tells part of our story. It holds our history, our heritage, and our beauty. There's no one 'right' skin color, texture, or look—just the one you were born to shine in. I hear that you're feeling unsure about your skin, and that's okay. But I want you to know that the world needs more people who look just like you. You are exactly as you're meant to be. There are a lot of kids who wished they were taller, or stronger, or had different skin, or had different hair color. But don't try and change yourself. You are unique just the way you are."

What Kids Say

"I have this mark on my face, and it makes me feel bad."

What I Say Back

"Thanks for telling me how you feel. That mark is just one small part of your skin story—it doesn't change all the amazing things about you. Everyone's skin is unique, and lots of people have birthmarks, freckles, or scars. Plus, puberty makes it so we have more pimples from time to time. Some people will notice it, and that's okay. What matters most is that you remember it doesn't take away from your worth or what your body can do."

* * * * *

When you have questions about your body, it's really important to talk to someone. Talk to your parents, your pediatrician, or a teacher at school. And remember, it's okay to feel bad about your body sometimes. Taking care of your body and yourself means learning how to respond to those questions, worries, and thoughts we have about our bodies with love and kindness. I'm here with you, every step of the way, and I believe in you—your one-of-a-kind body and all.

QUESTIONS I HAVE FOR MY PEDIATRICIAN

GLOSSARY

Acne: A word for pimples on the skin (also called zits). A common skin condition that happens when follicles under the skin become clogged.

Advocate: To stand up for someone or something

Androgens: A male sex hormone, like testosterone

Antioxidants: Compounds that help protect our cells from damage caused by harmful substances called *free radicals* and that keep our bodies functioning well

Attention-deficit/hyperactivity disorder (ADHD): A condition where a person has difficulty with attention or has hyperactivity/impulsivity that makes it hard for them to do what they need to do while at school, during play, or at home

Body hygiene and maintenance: Keeping yourself clean and cared for

Body mass index (BMI): A measurement that health professionals use as a "vital sign" of your health. A combination of your weight and your height without any heavy clothes or shoes on.

Body positivity advocate: Someone who stands up for others and for yourself when it comes to loving the bodies we're in

Bone marrow: The soft tissue in bones that makes stem cells

Bullying: When someone hurts another person on purpose—with words or actions—and keeps doing it even when it's clear that it's not funny

Calcium: An important mineral that makes it possible for your bones to grow

Carbohydrates: A type of macronutrient that gives us energy fast but doesn't last long in our bloodstream before it gets taken up by the body to be used and stored

Cardiologist: An expert in the human heart and in diseases like high cholesterol

Cells: The tons of little compartments that make up our bodies

Cerebral palsy: A medical condition that affects movement, muscle coordination, and posture

Character: Knowing what's right and wrong and sticking to your values

Cholesterol: A fatty substance in the blood

Chronic diseases: Diseases that affect you for a long time

Cisgender: A gender identity used to describe someone whose sex assigned at birth lines up with the gender they feel on the inside

Competence: Being really good at dealing with different situations and getting better by doing things and learning from them

Confidence: Really believing in yourself and what you're capable of

Connection: Having strong relationships with family, friends, school, and your community

Contribution: Understanding that you can make the world a better place as an individual

Control: Knowing that you can influence what happens based on your decisions

Coping: Being able to handle and deal with challenges in life using different strategies

Diabetes: A group of diseases that results in too much sugar in the blood

Dietitian: An expert in nutrition and the foods humans eat

DNA: The genetic code that makes up our genes

Eating disorder: When someone has unhealthy thoughts and behaviors about food and their body

Endocrinologist: An expert in human hormones and in diseases like diabetes

Environment: Everything in and around us

Epidermis: The top layer of your skin

Estrogen: A hormone made mostly in the ovaries

Fats: A type of macronutrient that is super-concentrated. Good for long-term energy and for energy storage.

Female: People who are born with a vulva. They usually have ovaries, a uterus, and certain genetics. These people are usually called *girls* at birth.

Fiber: A type of carbohydrate that our body can't digest. Fiber moves through our digestive tracks without getting broken down into sugar like other carbohydrates do.

Fixed mindset: Thinking that you have a set amount of intelligence or talent and there's not much you can do to change it

Free radicals: Substances that can damage cells in our bodies, causing illness and aging

Gastroenterologist: An expert in the body parts that make up your gut, like your intestines, your stomach, and your liver

Gender identity: What you feel and know you are—boy, girl, neither, or both—regardless of the body parts that you have

Genes: The building blocks of our bodies. Genes are made up of DNA.

Genitals: The body parts between your legs

Growth hormone: A hormone that stimulates the part of your bones responsible for making you taller

Growth mindset: Thinking about challenges and mistakes as opportunities to learn and become even better at something. Believing you can improve and get better at anything if you keep trying and learning.

Growth spurts: Fast jumps in height. These occur often in puberty.

Hair follicles: A tubelike structure that surrounds the root and strand of hair

Hormones: Chemicals in our bodies that travel through our bloodstream and deliver important messages to different parts of the body

Intersex: A sex other than male or female. This term is used when someone's body (inside parts or outside parts) doesn't fit into the typical male or female category.

Macronutrients: The main sources of energy our bodies need to function. Carbohydrates, protein, and fat are macronutrients.

Male: People who are born with a penis and who usually also have testicles and certain genetics. These people are usually called *boys* at birth.

Menstruation: When your body sheds the lining of the uterus (the inner part of a female reproductive system). Also called a period.

Mental health: Your overall well-being when it comes to how you think and feel

Mental health therapist: An expert in feelings and thoughts

Mental illness: A medical condition that affects a person's thoughts, mood, or behavior

Metabolism: The breakdown of food into energy for the body

Micronutrients: Nutrients our bodies need in smaller amounts compared with carbohydrates, proteins, and fats

Mindful self-compassion: Treating ourselves with kindness and understanding in the moment

Mindfulness: Paying attention to what's happening right now without getting caught up in worries about the past or the future. Keeping our minds where our bodies are.

Minerals: Elements that our bodies need for different processes, like making our muscles and nerves work

Nutrients: Substances the body needs to function properly

Parental controls: Limits on what's available to you based on your age or based on what your parents think is okay for you

Pediatrician: A medical practitioner specializing in children and their diseases

Period: When your body sheds the lining of the uterus (the inner part of a female reproductive system). Also called menstruation.

Personality: The characteristics, qualities, and/or traits that form your character

Physical therapist: An expert in body movement

Phytochemicals: Plant chemicals that help keep us healthy and strong and can help protect us from getting sick from diseases

Pimples: Another word for acne

Probiotics: Good bacteria that can help your body fight some infections

Proprioception: Your body's ability to tell where it is in space. Proprioception uses your eyes, your brain, and part of your inner ear.

Protein: A type of macronutrient. The building blocks of tissues, muscles, organs, enzymes, hormones, and the immune system.

Puberty: When a person starts changing from a kid into a teenager and, eventually, into an adult

Pubic area: The part of your body between your legs where your vulva or penis and scrotum are

Racism: When people aren't treated fairly because of their skin color or background

Red blood cells (RBCs): Cells that carry oxygen to all parts of your body

Resilience: Being able to bounce back from tough situations, even if it takes a lot of hard work

Sex assigned at birth: The label you were given at birth based on the body parts you have. Usually, sex is labeled based on whether babies have a vulva or a penis.

Sexism: When people think that one sex is better or more valuable than another sex

Sleep hygiene: The environment you sleep in and the way you prepare your body to fall asleep

Stimming: Short for self-stimulatory behaviors. Movements or sounds some people (especially those with autism) use to self-soothe or cope with sensory overload.

Temperament: The way you behave naturally or respond to the world around you

Testosterone: A hormone made by the testes that helps start puberty for children and teens with testes

Transgender: A gender identity used to describe someone whose gender they feel on the inside does not line up with their sex assigned at birth

Vital sign: Something doctors check, like your heartbeat or temperature, to see how your body is doing and if you're healthy

Vitamins: Nutrients that are critical for normal metabolism, growth, and development

Vulva: The area between the legs that includes the labia, vagina opening, urethra opening, and clitoris

Zits: Another word for acne

INDEX

T